· success with ·

science a... learners

Fay J Humphreys
and
John A Henderson

Blackie

ISBN 0 216 91902 9

First published 1986

Illustrated by Fay J Humphreys

Published by *Blackie and Son Limited*
Bishopbriggs, Glasgow G64 2NZ
7 Leicester Place London WC2H 7BP

British Library Cataloguing in Publication Data

Humphreys, Fay
Success with science early learners.
1. Science—Study and teaching
(Elementary)
I. Title II. Henderson, John
372.3′5 LB1585

ISBN 0-216-91902-9

Filmset by Advanced Filmsetters (Glasgow) Ltd
Printed in Great Britain by Thomson Litho Ltd,
East Kilbride, Scotland

contents

introduction

This book has been produced in order to fill a gap—a gap that exists before the introduction of 'formal' science programmes where skill and concept progression is achieved over a period of four or so years.

Infant teachers have traditionally found themselves 'out of it' as far as science is concerned. After all you can't do science with very young children anyway—or can you? The set of six **Science 'early learner' books** contains fundamental ideas and experiences to which young children will relate—written at their level in stories which they will read and enjoy. It is on to these experiences that we intend to build our science programme for the early stages.

For many teachers 'science' tends to be a daunting and offputting word. Many primary teachers feel inadequate since their last experience of science at school (or dare we say it, college!) was less than successful. What we hope to do here is dissolve some of the fears and give teachers sufficient confidence in their own innate (and usually underestimated) abilities which will enable them to follow this simple science programme, using materials and techniques both appropriate for, and readily available in, every infant classroom.

The infant classroom is one of the most fertile areas for scientific investigation. By its very nature it is laid out in a way which promotes investigative activities—the science that you do lies embedded in the work that you already do. We hope that in carrying out the activities in this book you will see links between your current classroom activities and what we are suggesting here, and will not feel threatened and insecure in the implementing of a 'science course' for infants.

Aims and objectives

In line with most science programmes for primary schools our aims are that the child should:

1 explore and gather experiences from his/her environment;
2 develop awareness, interest and concern for living things;
3 make observations and record results;
4 acquire knowledge and increase manipulative skills;
5 increase vocabulary and communication skills;
6 be able to pose questions and devise ways of problem solving.

In the main part of the text we have listed objectives for each of the topics. Frequently these will be achieved by carrying out several activities in the course.

Structure of the course

The book is divided into sections which match the divisions of the pupil material. These are: senses, water, heat, sound, moving and wheels.

Possible outcomes of the activities are mentioned although, please remember, we are all human and the occasional unexpected occurrence is bound to crop up. When it does it must be accepted as a valid outcome. After all, it happened so some explanation must be sought.

It is also important to highlight how these scientific activities link up with other areas of the curriculum. Again this cannot be a comprehensive review—more an awareness 'jogger'. The class teacher always sees far more by way of appropriate links for her class than an outsider ever will.

In listing resources we have tried to include absolutely everything that you will need for the successful implementation of each activity. Remember to check resource lists carefully before (days before) you are going to carry out the work. It may be that something has to be made up in advance, borrowed from a resource centre, prised out of an unwilling friend, relative or colleague, or even, as a last resort, purchased.

Although a suggested sequence of experiments (sorry, activities) is indicated, it is not prescriptive (though strongly recommended in the case of Water). You may wish to organize the activities in a different order to suit your own particular needs and aptitudes. The timescale is relatively unimportant. An investigation lasts as long as it needs to, and more importantly, as long as it interests the children.

Also, remember this is a book for teachers and that the language is for teachers. We would not expect words like 'opaque', 'translucent' or 'transparent' to appear in word banks or lists. A more appropriate terminology for the pupils would be:

'Things we can't see through'
'When we look through these, things look funny'
'Things we can see through'.

The introductory notes at the beginning of each section are intended to help you, the teacher, they are not part of the pupils' course and should not be taught to them.

Science is fun. In the infant room it's great fun so go ahead and enjoy it!

senses

It is of supreme importance that all living things, including ourselves, are aware of what is happening in their environment. How do you survive in a changing environment if you cannot detect the changes? Our environment has two components, an internal and an external one, and we must be able to respond to each. Our internal environment cannot, and let's face it, need not, be considered within the context of infant science but our external environment—what is going on around us—is of paramount importance. For a young child 'I' is the most important word and therefore how 'I' fit in to 'my' world is an ideal starting point.

We detect and respond to our environment by using our senses. So do all other animals. So does Rosie in the story book. Something which is of interest to you (and possibly to your children) is the first sense that Rosie uses in the story. Rosie hears the gate go 'click'. Probably a dog's most important senses are hearing and smell, but it is not so with humans. Had it been a human child waiting for some one to come home, she would have been 'watching'. Animals, other than ourselves, detect their environment by using touch and taste and smell to a very much greater extent than we do. Discussion with the children about their pets, or indeed watching a class pet like a hamster or gerbil, will bring this fact to light. If such an animal is placed in a new environment it spends a lot of time exploring and 'getting to know' its new environment by sniffing, tasting and smelling. Sight, however, is our most important sense.

As has been mentioned in the Introduction, the sequence in which the topics are dealt with is not terribly important. If you wish to follow the story with a scientific follow-up activity, obviously you will start with 'hearing'. If not, you might wish to start with 'sight'.

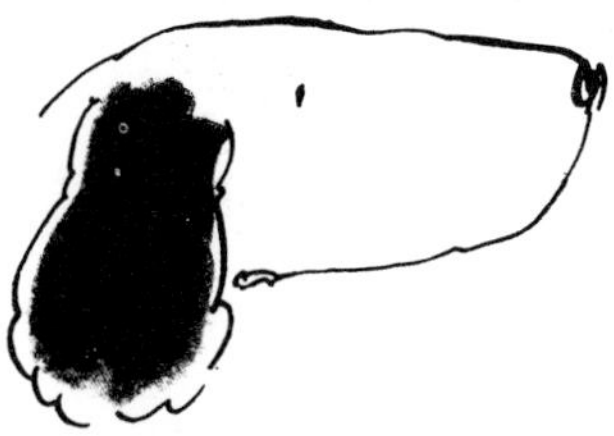

Sight

In order to see, we need light and eyes. First let us explore light.

Light is a form of radiation which tends to be produced by relatively hot objects like the sun, a fire, or an electric lamp. However, the majority of objects we see do not, in themselves, produce light—they merely reflect it. If you are outside during the daytime the chances are that the only source of light around is the sun. It follows that everything you look at must be reflecting some sunlight into your eyes and it is this reflected sunlight which makes objects visible. Imagine the same scene at night with no moon or street lights to help.

Light travels in straight lines and it is this property which makes shadows—an endless source of fun for children. Mirrors also depend on the way in which light travels in straight lines in order to produce images. If the mirrors are curved, however, they modify the light path and we see things distorted, reduced in size, or even turned upside-down.

Shaped blocks of glass or clear plastic also modify the light which travels through them, e.g. magnifying glasses and other types of lenses.

Eyes are detectors of light and different animals have eyes which are adapted to different needs. Dogs and cats, for example, do not have colour vision and some birds, fish and insects only have partial colour vision. Predators tend to have their eyes placed together at the front of their head so that they have good binocular, three-dimensional vision which is essential for judging distance and allowing them to catch their prey. On the other hand, the animals which are usually hunted tend to have eyes placed on the sides of their heads so that they have good all-round vision to warn them of the presence and approach of predators.

The activities which follow introduce some of these ideas to the children.

In daytime all light comes from the sun

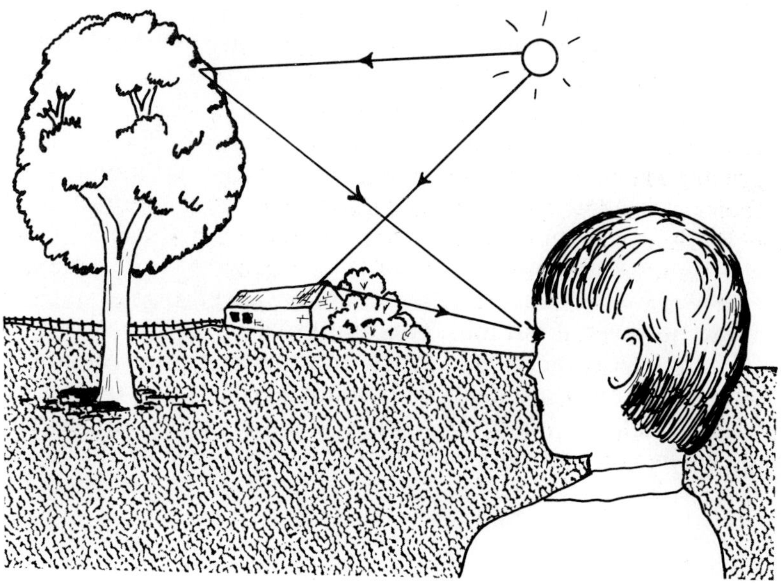

Objective: The pupils will be aware that light is needed for seeing.

RESOURCES

1 A light-tight box with peephole—see Appendix 1 for details of construction.
2 A collection of various objects with which the pupils are familiar. These should be easily recognizable and small enough to fit into one end of the light-tight box.

ACTIVITY SE1

Select one of the objects and, without the children seeing it, place it in the box then close the lid. The children now take it in turn to look through the peephole and describe what they see. If the box has been well constructed and the child's eye is close to the peephole he should not be able to see anything. Replies like 'Nothing' or 'Blackness' might be expected. (If the lid is a loose fit or the peephole is too big it might be possible to see a vague shape or outline.)

Now remove the lid while the child is looking through the peephole. What does he see now?

Repeat the activity, not necessarily immediately, with different objects.

With very young children the activity should be left at this stage. With older pupils it should be possible to continue with questions like:

'Why do you see the object?'
'What gets into the box so that you can see the object?'
'Would this work in a dark room? Why not?'
'Would it work at night?'

Children using a light-tight box

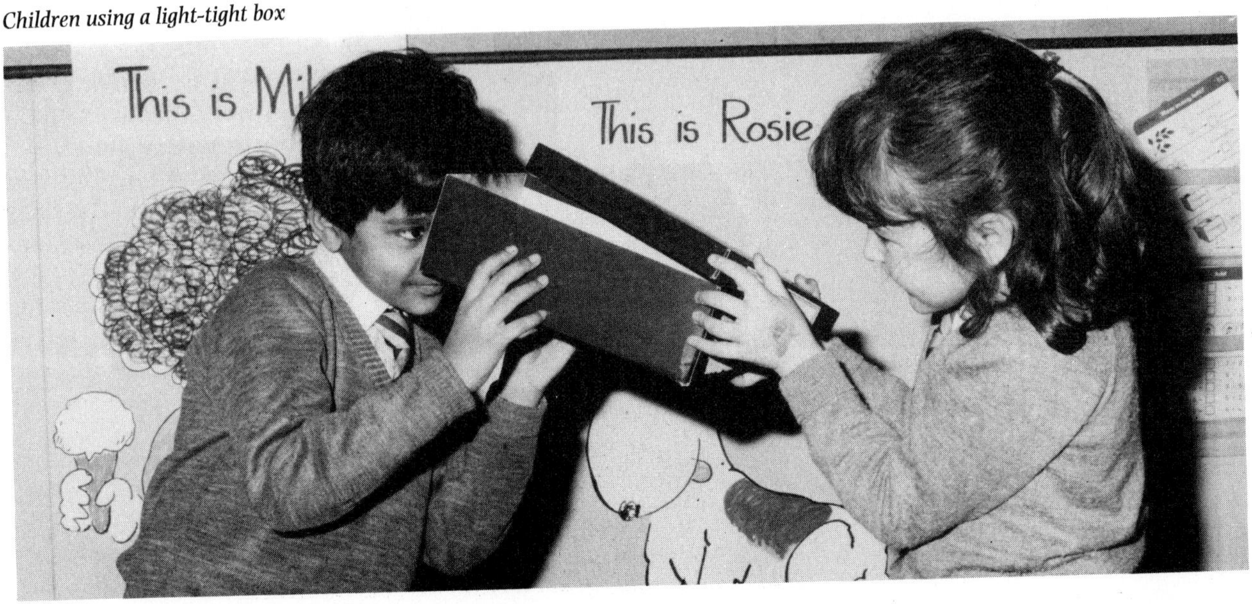

LINKING ACTIVITIES: Art

1 Draw what you see in the dark box.
2 Draw what you see in the lit box.

ACTIVITY SE2

RESOURCES

None.

Discuss with the class, or a small group, what it is like if they wake up during the night. Can they see anything? If not, why not?

As a follow-up find out how many have 'night lights' of one sort or another left on. Emphasize that it is not childish or cowardly to have such lights.

LINKING ACTIVITIES: Mathematics

Count the number with night lights and the number without then use the results to produce pictograms.

ACTIVITY SE3

RESOURCES

None.

Discuss the difference between day and night. What is it like at night with no street lighting?

LINKING ACTIVITIES: Language/Art

1 Make up, and tell, stories about being out at night.
2 Make up a class poem entitled 'Feeling at Night'.
3 Draw 'night' pictures.

Wall display of class poem

A pupil's 'night picture'

Objective: The pupils will be aware of shadows.

RESOURCES

1 An overhead projector or a slide projector.
2 A blank wall.

ACTIVITY SE4

Place the projector so that it produces a brightly lit square on the wall reaching from floor level upwards. The pupils can now walk, stand, play or move about in the space between the projector and the wall and observe the shadows which they produce. They should be encouraged to notice the shapes they make and to try to produce effects like two-headed bodies or people with four arms and so on.

Place the children between the OHP and the wall

RESOURCES

1 An overhead projector or a slide projector.
2 A blank wall.
3 Black sugar paper.
4 A pencil.
5 Scissors.

ACTIVITY SE5

Place the projector so that it produces a brightly lit square on the wall reaching from floor level upwards. Stick a piece of black paper on the wall then have a pupil cast a shadow, e.g. a profile, on the paper. Draw round the outline then cut out the shape of the shadow.

LINKING ACTIVITIES: Art/Mathematics/Games

1 Produce a large wall frieze of a group of pupils or of the entire class.
2 Compare the sizes of individuals using the cut-out shadow shapes. (This assumes that complete full-sized figures have been produced.)
3 Games like 'shadow tag' could be played.

RESOURCES

1 An overhead projector or a slide projector.
2 A blank wall.

ACTIVITY SE6

Place the projector so that it produces a brightly lit square on the wall reaching from floor level upwards. Place pupils of the same height at different distances from the wall and note how their shadows are different heights.

Can the pupils devise a way of making a small pupil look as big as a tall pupil (or even as big as the teacher)?

Children at different distances from OHP

LINKING ACTIVITIES: Language

Ask the pupils for words describing size: 'big', 'small', bigger', 'smaller' and so on.

RESOURCES

1 An overhead projector.
2 Figures, from a well-known picture book, traced onto paper and then cut out. The figures should be small enough to fit on the stage of the OHP.

ACTIVITY SE7

Tell the story using the shadows produced by the OHP to illustrate the action.

EXTENSION ACTIVITY

The children can write their own story, produce the cutouts and tell the story themselves, using the OHP (perhaps even using recorded sound effects).

RESOURCES

1 A bright, sunny day.
2 Lots of time.
3 Chalk.

ACTIVITY SE8

Start early in the day, or better still, in the afternoon of the day before and place pupils in the playground so that they cast shadows. Draw round the shadow outlines with chalk. Repeat the activity at, or around, midday and, if time (and sunshine) permits, later in the afternoon.

Draw attention to the different positions of the shadows. Do the children notice that the shadows of the same person change in length depending on the time of day? Can they work out what has taken the place of the projector that was used in Activities SE4, 5, 6 and 7?

Note the 3 o'clock shadow from the day before

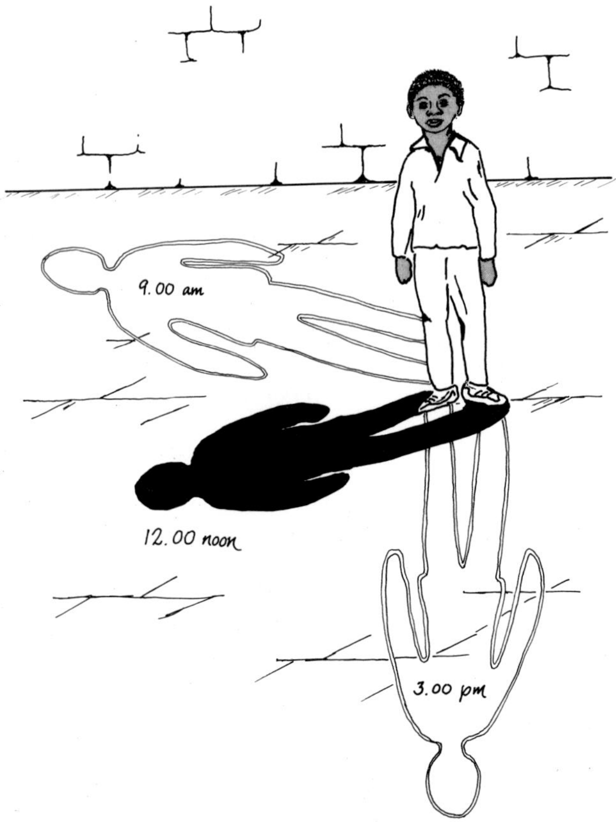

Objective: Pupils will be aware of the difference between transparent, translucent and opaque materials.

Note While the pupils will be aware of the different materials and their properties, the words 'transparent', 'translucent' and 'opaque' should not be given to them at this stage.

RESOURCES

Prepare several tubes (kitchen roll centres) each with a different material over one end so that some are transparent, some are translucent and some are opaque.

Materials which could be used are:

OHP acetate cellophane clear plastic	transparent
tissue paper greaseproof-paper plastic from sandwich box	translucent
thick card wood aluminium foil	opaque

ACTIVITY SE9

The children look out of the window through various tubes in turn and describe what they see. Depending on the material the responses should vary from 'Nothing' to 'A bright spot' or 'A sort of shape' to 'What is outside the window'.

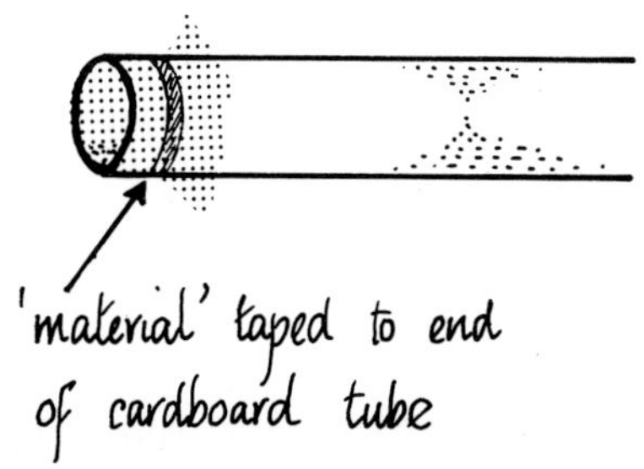

Viewing tube made from a cardboard tube

RESOURCES

Samples of materials which are translucent, transparent or opaque.

ACTIVITY SE10

Give the pupils samples of material and ask them to sort them into three groups: 'Can see through clearly', 'Can't see through at all' or 'Can see something through'.

LINKING ACTIVITY: Mathematics

Sorting and sets.

Objective: The pupils will be aware of different colours.

RESOURCES

Prepare a selection of brightly-coloured objects, each only one colour. The colour should be selected with the pupils' abilities in mind and only definite colours—red, green, yellow, etc., used. Avoid turquoise, magenta, burnt sienna and so on.

ACTIVITY SE11

The following sequence is a progression of small activities which teach and reinforce the recognition and naming of colours.

1 From the assorted objects the pupil must select two which are of the same colour. Either the pupil or the teacher should then name the colour.
2 From the assorted objects the pupil selects one which is the same colour as a specified one. The teacher names the colour as the specified one is held up.
3 As each object is held up the pupil names the colour. This could be turned into a team game.
4 The pupil selects an object with a named colour.
5 One pupil names a colour and the next has to select an object of that colour.
6 Play a game of 'I Spy . . .' using colours instead of first letters, i.e. 'I spy with my little eye something which is . . . red.'

Objective: The pupils will be aware that a transparent material can modify the appearance of an object viewed through it.

RESOURCES

A selection of transparent (clear) objects like: OHP acetate, magnifying glass, old spectacles, drinking glass, bottle, etc.

ACTIVITY SE12

The pupils look at an object first of all directly, then through one of the transparent objects. Does the object look different? If so, how? Draw a 'before and after' pair of pictures.

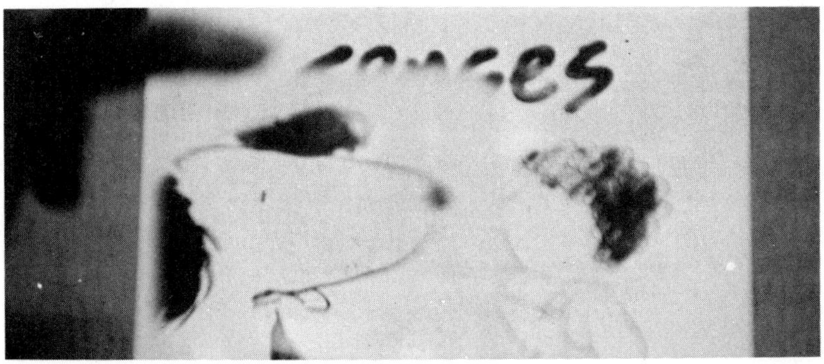

Looking through a transparent material

RESOURCES

1 A collection of coloured objects. Stick to dense, simple colours like red, green and blue.
2 A 'colour mask'. Instructions for making this are in Appendix 2.

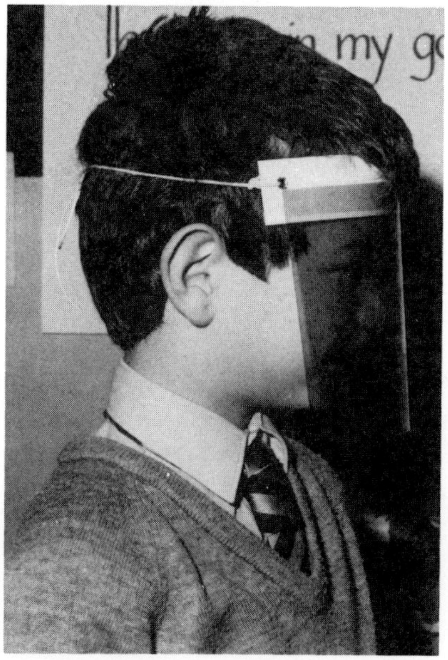

Child wearing a 'colour mask'

ACTIVITY SE13

Place the mask over a child's eyes then ask him to identify the various objects by naming their colour or to name the colour of a selected object.

ACTIVITY SE14

While wearing the mask the pupil should look at the various objects and try to describe the colour of each one in turn. The objects can then be looked at without the mask and the difference in colour noted.

OUTCOMES

The results obtained in Activities SE13 and SE14 will be very dependent on the colour and quality of the material used to make the mask. Ideally the coloured acetate should be very dense in colour and either red, blue or green. The coloured acetate acts as a filter and will only allow through light of its own colour. So, a red object viewed through a red filter will appear red but, if the object is green or blue then no light will pass through the filter and the object will appear black. Of course, it is most unlikely that the coloured objects will be pure in colour and the filter will almost certainly be imperfect but the results will be similar to those described.

Objective: The pupils will be aware of the effect of a mirror (reflection).

RESOURCES

A large mirror.

ACTIVITY SE15

Hang up the mirror in the classroom where the children will be able to see themselves (and each other). Leave the mirror for some time and casually encourage the children to use it.

RESOURCES

1 A small mirror for each pupil involved in the activity.
2 A bright, sunny day (or the light from a projector).

ACTIVITY SE16

Position the children so that their mirrors catch the light from the window (or the projector). Show them how to reflect the light on to the ceiling and walls in the classroom then allow them to enjoy themselves for some time. Where does the light on the ceiling come from? How does it get up there?

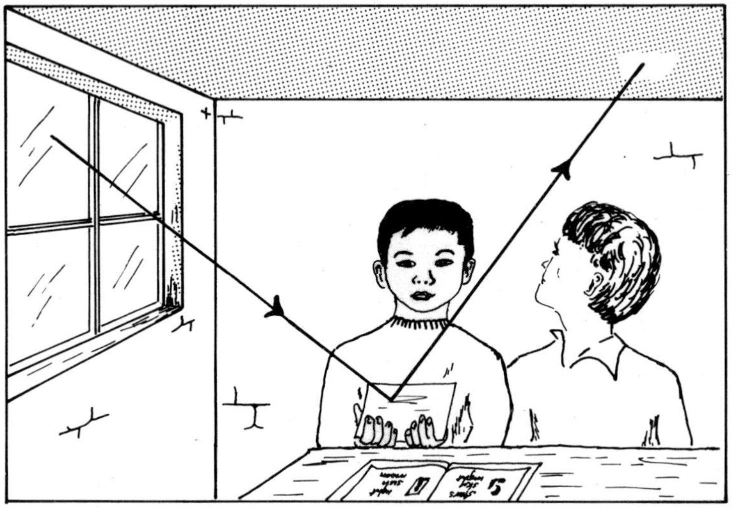

Light path from sun to mirror and mirror to ceiling

RESOURCES

1 A small, flat mirror for each pupil.
2 A concave and a convex mirror for each pupil. The easiest, and cheapest way of obtaining these is to raid the school dining room for a quantity of highly-polished chrome-plated pudding spoons.

ACTIVITY SE17

The children should look at themselves first of all in the plain mirror and then in the two curved surfaces of the spoon. (Be prepared for a great deal of hilarity and excitement.) When they have settled down again ask them to draw themselves as they appear in the two surfaces of the spoon and also in the ordinary mirror.

The curved surface of a spoon will distort your reflection!

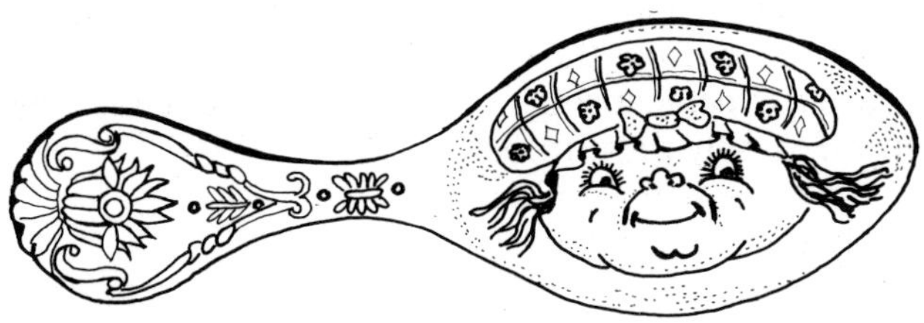

'Spoon drawings'

OUTCOMES

Activity SE17 is great fun. The resulting drawings show just how observant young children can be. The convex surface will make them look smaller and thinner while the concave surface will make them look fatter if they are close to it but if they hold it far away they will be smaller and upside-down.

LINKING ACTIVITY: Language/Observation

1 For example, poems like:

Before I take my pudding
I always look to see
If someone in my pudding spoon
Is really, really me.

For up and down I am so thin
And sideways I'm so fat.
I really can't believe it's true
That I could look like that!
(Anon.)

2 Collect 'funny mirror' lists. Include things like: wing mirrors on cars, sides of polished kettles, shop mirrors (for spotting thieves), etc.

Objective: The pupils will be aware of the effect of a simple magnifying lens.

RESOURCES

1 A magnifying glass—preferably of the type which has legs holding it at the correct distance from the table to ensure correct focusing (Osmiroid supply these under their catalogue name 'LEM').
2 A variety of very small objects.

ACTIVITY SE18

The children should be allowed to examine the small objects without, and with, the aid of the magnifying glass. Encourage them to think of small objects to examine. Ask them to bring things into the class. They can record their observations by drawing what they see.

Pupils using a magnifying glass

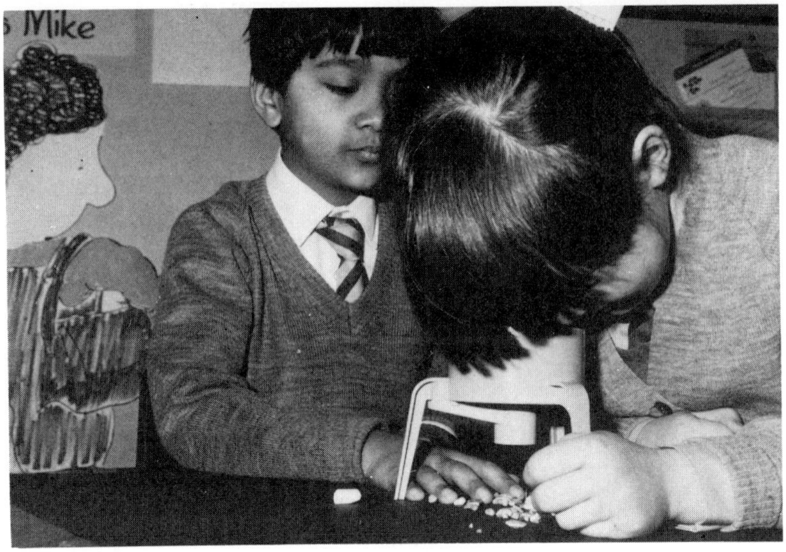

Note If the pupils use the lens like a telescope do not stop them. They will find out for themselves that it does not work this way.

Objective: The pupils will be aware that there are different kinds of eyes.

RESOURCES

The pupils.

ACTIVITY SE19

Eyes come in all shapes and sizes, so start with an eye survey. How many eyes are there in the classroom?

*LINKING ACTIVITIES: **Mathematics***

Eye 'counters' can be made in different colours of card (blue, green, brown and black) and used for sticking on block graphs.

RESOURCES

Various pets and small animals and/or slides of animals showing their eyes. (A set of such slides is available from H & H Productions.)

ACTIVITY SE20

Look at the different kinds of eyes (stick to vertebrates to begin with). Do they all look alike? What do they all have in common?

OUTCOMES

You should find that all vertebrates have two eyes but within the vertebrate groups you will notice:

1 no eyelids on fish;
2 eyelashes on mammals;
3 they all have a dark coloured central part (the pupil).

*LINKING ACTIVITIES: **Language development***

'With my eyes I can see . . .' a development of 'I spy with my little eye'. Try playing this pretending you are a rabbit or a mouse or a cat.

ACTIVITY SE21

How do different animals view the world? A useful video tape is available which shows the same route being explored by a child, a grown-up and a small dog. The video tape is available, in VHS format only, from H & H Productions.

Objective: The pupils will be aware that there are different colours of eyes.

RESOURCES

The pupils.

ACTIVITY SE22

What colours are the eyes of the children? Make lists of different eye colours. This can be more difficult than you might imagine and sometimes you have to compromise with the hazels and topaz which some may suggest.

*LINKING ACTIVITIES: **Mathematics***

Eye counters again. Number work.

RESOURCES

The pupils.

ACTIVITY SE23

Make a block graph of the principal eye colours in the class.

Warning! Don't fall into the genetics game trap—'What colour are Daddy's eyes?' etc. You can end up with some nasty, unanswerable questions that way.

Objective: The pupils will be aware that different animals have eyes in different positions.

RESOURCES

1 The pupils.
2 A rabbit or a mouse (or pictures of a rabbit or a mouse).

'Hunted'—eyes on sides of head

ACTIVITY SE24

Look carefully at the rabbit or mouse. How do its eyes differ in position from yours (or a cat's)?

OUTCOMES

The rabbit and mouse, and indeed all grazing and plant-eating mammals, have eyes positioned on either side of the head. This gives them maximum peripheral vision—extremely important if you are likely to become the dinner of one of the hunting animals.

On the other hand, the hunter has to have precise vision to be able to judge distances accurately. When he pounces he must not miss. This is achieved by possessing binocular vision, i.e. the two eyes are sited on the head so that the owner can look at an object with both eyes at the same time and thus accurately assess distance.

RESOURCES

1 The pupils.
2 Cat and mouse masks, if desired. See Appendix 3 for instructions.

ACTIVITY SE25

Play the 'Cat and Mouse' game. Divide the class into two groups—cats and mice. The cats line up against one wall and the mice along the opposite wall. One mouse is placed in the middle of the area facing the other mice and with her back to the cats. This mouse is not allowed to turn round or to move her head. She must look forward at all times. One of the cats is chosen, without the mouse knowing which one it is. This cat has to stalk the mouse in an attempt to catch it. The mouse cannot run away until she sees the cat. If the mouse is caught try again with another mouse, and cat, until all the children have had a turn. Record the number of 'mouse escapes' and 'mouse catches'. (This should be heavily biased in favour of 'mouse catches'.)

Now 'design' a mouse using two children standing back-to-back so that they are looking out sideways, just as a real mouse does. Once again this mouse must not move her head, but now see how often the mouse can escape. (The first half of the mouse to spot the cat immediately tells the other and both run off.)

Look at the picture of the mouse on page 20. Why is there one eye on each side of her head?

'Cats' and 'mice'

LINKING ACTIVITIES: Language/Drama/Art

1 Collect, and tell, cat and mouse stories.
2 Act out the 'Cat and Mouse' game with special attention to cat movement/mouse movement.
3 Make cat and mouse masks for the children to wear when playing the game.

RESOURCES

1 Slides and/or pictures of invertebrate eyes.
2 Live invertebrate material.
Note The location of the school will determine what live material is available but remember that most invertebrates are much safer to handle than vertebrates. So grit your teeth and collect spiders and slugs, flies and earthworms and make as large an 'eye collection' as you can.
3 Magnifiers.

ACTIVITY SE26

The children should look at, and draw, the 'eyes of the world'.

Note Since one of our aims must always be to foster a respect for life remember that these animals will be temporary visitors and should be returned to their own homes after they have helped us in our search.

We cannot start emphasizing this aspect of conservation early enough. Young children do not fear or try to destroy living things until Mummy (or teacher) says, 'Take that nasty, dirty spider (worm, slug, fly) out of my sight.'

OUTCOMES

Viewing a collection of invertebrate eyes will provide all sorts of new information. For example, some animals have eyes on stalks. Some animals have lots of eyes. Others have eyes which cover most of their heads. This can lead to all sorts of discussion about where they live, what they need to see, etc.

The diagram on page 20 shows sketches of most of the eye types that you are likely to encounter. Don't replicate it for class use. Let the children make their own drawings of the animals.

LINKING ACTIVITY: Art/Language

1 Invertebrates through magnifiers—make 'monsters'.
2 Spider poem (or whatever 'creepy crawlie' is most popular with the class).

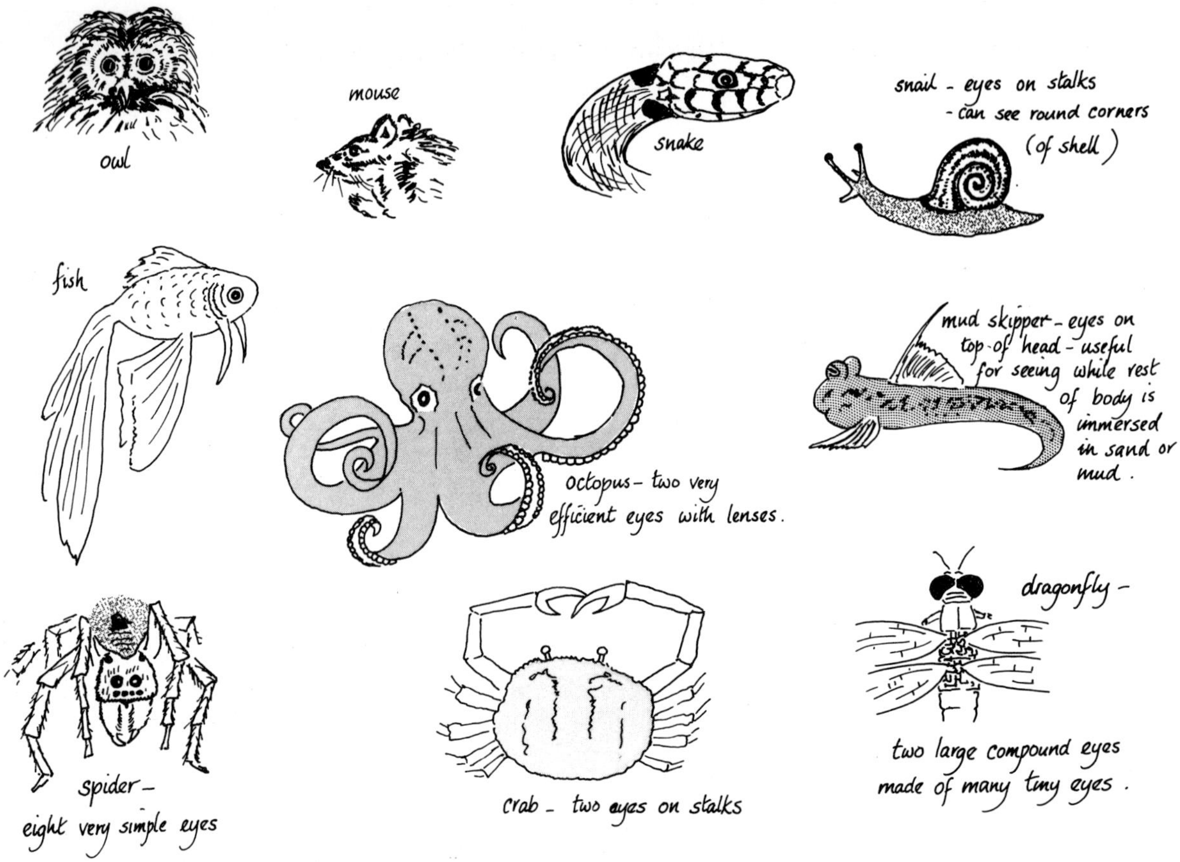

Various 'eye types'

Hearing

The basic information that you will require prior to starting this section on hearing will be found in the chapter on sound, pages 44 to 52.

Objective: To show pupils they can discriminate between the sounds produced by different things and can thus identify them.

RESOURCES

An audio tape of sound effects. (A suitable tape is available from H & H Productions.)

ACTIVITY SE27

This activity can be carried out as a competition between different groups in the class, as a class activity or as an individual activity. Play each effect on the tape and see how many pupils can identify the sounds correctly.

*LINKING ACTIVITY: **Language***

'Collect' words which describe the sounds which are heard on the tape.

RESOURCES

1 An audio cassette recorder.
2 A microphone.
3 An audio cassette.

ACTIVITY SE28

Prepare a recording of the children's voices. Each child should read or say the same thing. Play the recordings back to the children but in a different order from the original recording order. Can they recognize all the voices—especially their own?

RESOURCES

1 A blindfold.
2 Several children.

ACTIVITY SE29

Blindfold one of the group (or get him to stand with his back to the rest of the group). Each member of the group should speak in turn and the blindfolded member has to guess who it is.

Objective: To make the pupils aware that one of their ears might be better at hearing than the other.

RESOURCES

1 A quiet room (or playground).
2 A clock which ticks.
3 Some way of marking positions on the floor (counters or pieces of paper).

ACTIVITY SE30

One of the children stands in the middle of the space while another moves away on his left-hand side carrying the clock. When the first child can no longer hear the clock he tells the 'clock carrier' to stop. With his eyes closed, and his right hand covering his right ear, he has to listen carefully as the clock is brought nearer. As soon as he hears the clock he calls 'Stop'. The position of the clock is marked on the floor.

The same procedure is carried out to test his right ear.

Are both distances the same? What does it mean if they are? What does it mean if they are not?

Pupils carrying out 'hearing' experiment

Objective: To make the pupils aware that not all people hear equally well.

RESOURCES

1 A quiet room (or playground).
2 A clock which ticks.
3 Some way of marking positions on the floor (counters or pieces of paper).

ACTIVITY SE31

This is basically the same as Activity SE30 except instead of using different ears from the same pupil different pupils are used.

ACTIVITY SE32

The same procedure is followed as in Activity SE31 but this time the different people should be older (Primary 6 or 7 pupils), elderly (young staff members) and ancient (anyone over 25).

OUTCOMES

A difference in the sensitivity of each ear is to be expected but should not be too pronounced. As the owners of ears become more mature the ears tend to respond less well, especially to high frequency sounds. This drop off is to be expected and should not cause any alarm—despondency, perhaps, but not alarm—it's quite normal!

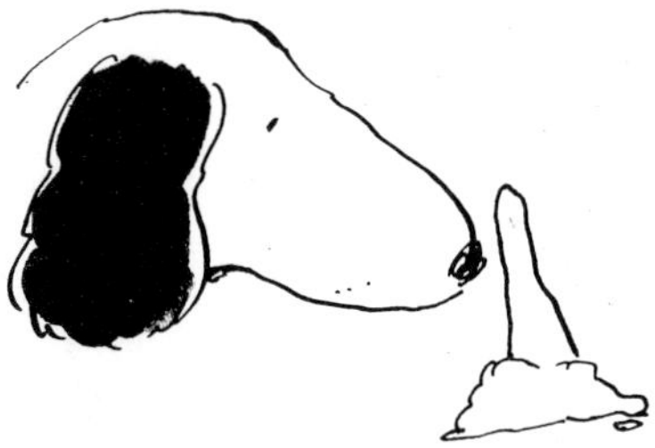

Smell, taste and touch

Warning! Avoid dangerous chemicals like ammonia, bleach, petrol, dry cleaning fluid and nail polish remover.

Objective: The pupils will be aware that many substances can be identified by smell.

RESOURCES

Small, covered containers (with lids) containing a variety of household materials. Miniature jam pots are ideal for this since they can be cleaned thoroughly before adding the material in question. A piece of gauze stretched over the top is useful since it does not allow spillage of the contents when the lid is off. Possible contents are: orange segment, soap, spices, apple, banana, onion, cheese, curry, fish, TCP, crisps and so on.

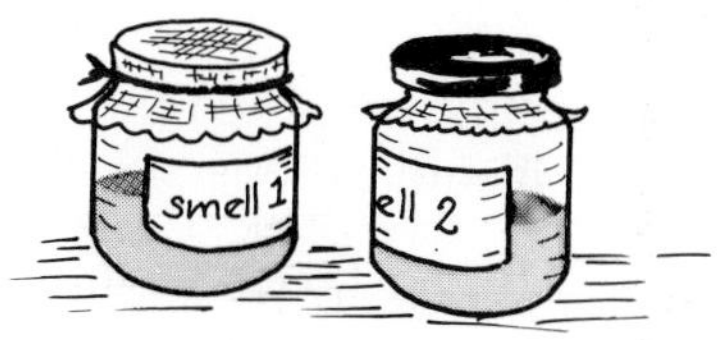

Gauze covered 'smelling' jars

ACTIVITY SE33

With the lid removed each child is allowed a 3 second sniff of each jar.

Working in groups there can be an element of competition to see which group can identify most of the substances.

Discuss with the class:
'Rosie smells the ice cream with her nose. It smells good.'
Questions arising directly from this are:

'What smells do we like?'
'What smells do we not like?'
'Have some things no smell at all?'
'Do things always smell the same?'

We can use our noses to tell if something has gone bad. (Don't do this practically.)

Pupils sniffing jars

Objective: The pupils will be aware that our sense of taste discriminates between only very large, major divisions.

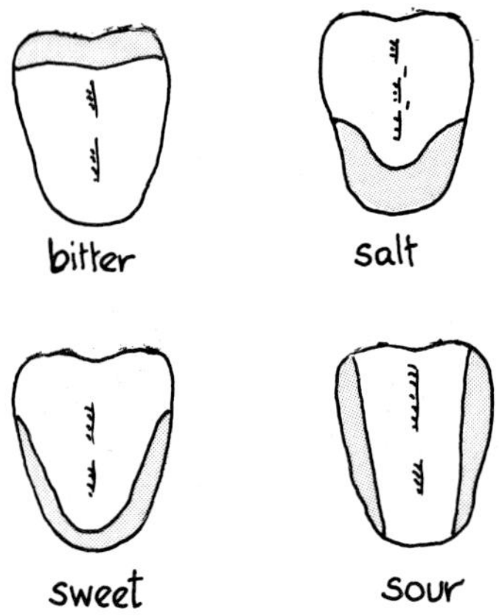

Taste zones of the tongue

Our tongue is only capable of discriminating between four major tastes. These are salty, sweet, sour and bitter. A different part of the tongue's surface detects each of these tastes and it is possible, by experiment, to isolate these areas. This is far too complicated to expect young children to attempt—the difference between bitter and sour is beyond most of them anyway.

The ability to discriminate between the vast number of flavours that we come across depends on our sense of smell. This is why most food is considered to be so tasteless when one has a stuffed-up nose as the result of a head cold.

'Rosie tastes the ice cream with her tongue.
Rosie likes the taste of ice cream.'

Popular ice cream flavours seem an obvious follow up to this part of the story. Most children are adamant about what they like and dislike, but can they really tell them apart? They all agree emphatically that they can tell the difference, so put them to the test. This gives an extremely popular activity for pupils (and staff).

RESOURCES

1 Tubs of ice cream of several different flavours. It is best if these are all homogeneous with no 'lumpy bits'.
2 Plastic teaspoons or lolly sticks (enough for 1 per pupil per flavour).

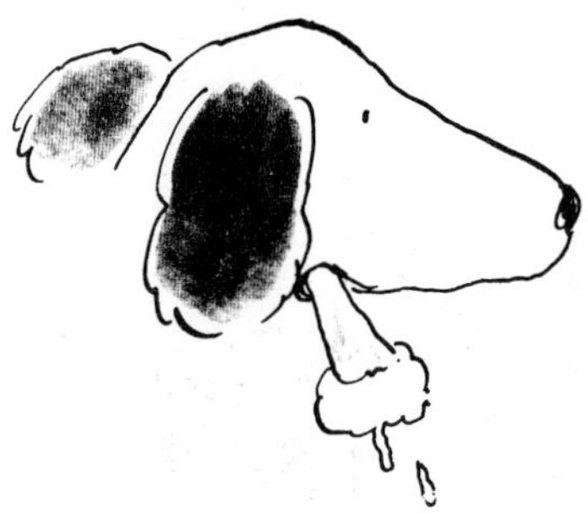

ACTIVITY SE34

Each child, in turn, is brought out to be 'tested'. The pupil stands with her back to the teacher and the tubs of ice cream and then closes her eyes and holds her nose. A small quantity of one flavour of ice cream is inserted in her mouth. Can she name the flavour? She is now tested with another flavour without telling her if her first guess is correct. When she has completed the test she can be told the number of correct identifications she has managed.

It is essential to alternate the flavours and order of presentation from pupil to pupil otherwise they soon memorize the correct sequence.

If you feel this is going to be messy and awkward then it is possible to substitute crisps of different flavours for the ice cream and do away with the teaspoons.

Tasting ice cream

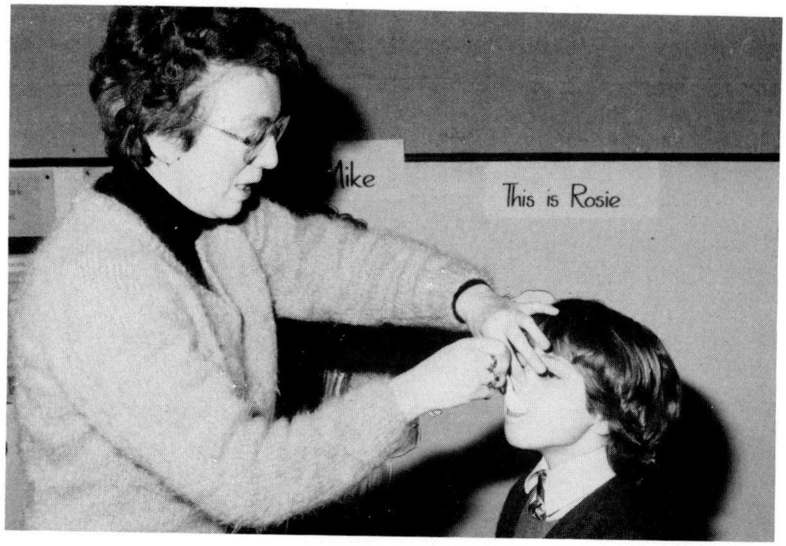

Note Before starting the next three activities with very young children it may be necessary to discuss and explain the terms rough/smooth, soft/hard and hot/cold. This can be done, for example, using a discovery table or by class discussion.

Objective: The pupils will be able to discriminate between rough and smooth.

RESOURCES

1 A large cardboard box with two arm holes cut in the side and a lid which can be closed.
2 A collection of about 12 to 18 objects some with rough surfaces the rest smooth.

ACTIVITY SE35

Place the objects in the box then close the lid. Each child is asked to sort the objects into two groups, putting all the smooth ones at one end and the rough ones at the other.

A 'feely' box

Objective: The pupils will be able to discriminate between hard and soft.

RESOURCES

1 A large cardboard box with two arm holes cut in the side and a lid which can be closed.
2 A collection of about 12 to 18 objects, some hard and the rest soft.

ACTIVITY SE36

Place the objects in the box then close the lid. Each child is asked to sort the objects into two groups, putting all the hard ones at one end and the soft ones at the other.

LINKING ACTIVITY

A class chart of 'Rough', 'Smooth', 'Hard', 'Soft' can be assembled, and left over a period of time for additions.

Objective: The pupils will be able to discriminate between hot and cold.

RESOURCES

1 Two similar containers for water.
2 Hot water. This should be hot but not too hot.
3 Cold water.
4 A cardboard box with arm holes cut in the side.

ACTIVITY SE37

Three-quarter fill one of the containers with hot water and put the same amount of cold water in the other container.

Place the containers in the box so that the pupil carrying out the activity will not be able to see which one is which. She should now test how hot or cold the water is by using her fingers—either the same finger in each container in turn, or fingers of both hands simultaneously.

Vary the position of the containers from time to time so that the children cannot just remember the answer from the previous pupil's attempt.

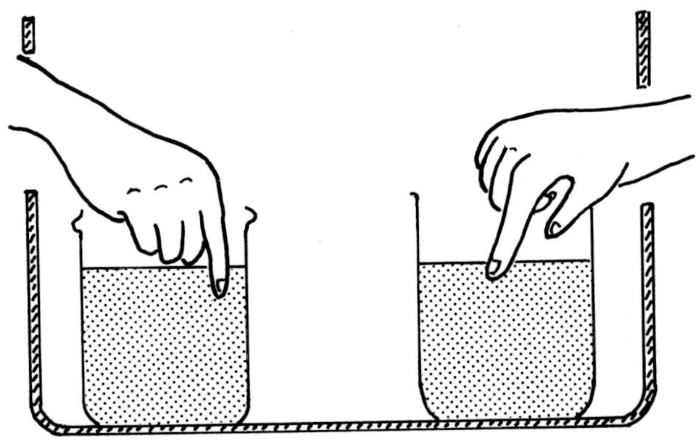

Can we discriminate between hot and cold?

Objective: The pupils will be aware that they can identify objects by their shape.

RESOURCES

1 A variety of well-known objects, such as toys and equipment, from the classroom.
2 Several cloth, or opaque plastic bags (the 'feely bag').

ACTIVITY SE38

Put one object in each bag which is then sealed. The children have to discover, by feel, the identity of each object.

This activity can easily be turned into a game or competition.

Objective: Pupils will be aware that they can feel pain.

Note It is considered inadvisable to attempt any practical activities associated with this objective.

Discussion of incidents like, in our story, Mike's falling and hurting his knee will give rise, as you well know, to a spontaneous list of similar incidents, ranging from the trivial to the bizarre, all of which have happened to one or other member of the class.

water

Introduction

The basic concepts involved in understanding topics like floating and sinking include: volume, mass, density, force, pressure and conservation of volume. All of these concepts are far too advanced for pupils in the early stages of the primary school. Indeed, some of them are so complex that many people never fully grasp them. It is for this reason that the ideas involved should be introduced early in life through play. The activities described in this section are intended to start the pupil on the long road of discovery which may ultimately lead to an understanding of that most difficult, yet simplest, of principles— the Principle of Archimedes.

The concepts are essential for a full understanding of much of science as it applies to everyday life and we must expect that it will take years of experiencing applications of these concepts before they can be grasped completely by the pupils. The earlier these experiences are started the easier, and quicker, will be the understanding of such concepts. However, in order to ensure the formulation of well-founded concepts it is essential that misleading information and ideas are kept to a minimum. The activities, and resources for them, have been carefully thought out and chosen to ensure that this minimum is achieved. The order of carrying out the activities is important. The objectives form a progression as do the activities for any one objective.

Objective: The pupils will be aware that water takes up the shape of the vessel into which it is poured.

RESOURCES

1 Several translucent containers of different shapes.
2 Water.
3 A 'wet area' for working in.
4 Protective clothing for the pupils (and teacher).

ACTIVITY W1

The pupils should be encouraged to fill one container from another. No attempt should be made to draw any conclusions from the results of this activity. Essentially this is just water play and should be left at that level. As the pupils' understanding develops it may be possible to draw attention to the way in which water changes shape depending on the shape of the container or how, sometimes, water will overflow when a small vessel is filled from a large one. However, this should not be forced, for some pupils it could well take years for the idea to formulate.

*LINKING ACTIVITY: **Poem by Rodney Bennett***

Water in bottles
Water in pans
Water in kettles
Water in cans
It is always the shape
Of whatever it's in
Bucket or kettle
Or bottle or tin.

Pupils working in the 'wet area'

Objective A: The pupils will be aware that if an object is placed in water, some of the water will be displaced.

Objective B: The pupils will be aware that the water level in a vessel will rise when an object is placed in it.

RESOURCES

1 A bucket or similar container for water.
2 A basin to stand the bucket in.
3 Water.
4 A variety of solid objects which will go into the bucket and have a volume between a quarter and a half of the bucket's volume.
5 A 'wet area' to work in.
6 Protective clothing.

ACTIVITY W2

Place the bucket in the basin and fill the bucket to the brim with water. Gently place one of the objects into the water. What happens to the water? Why does some spill out? Remember Albert and Harry!

Repeat the procedure with other objects, remembering to empty the basin and refill the bucket each time.

Bucket filled to brim with water

OUTCOMES

The volume of water displaced should be exactly equal to the volume of the part of the object which is immersed. In practice, however, this does not always appear to happen. Sometimes, if enough care is not exercised, extra water spills out and, on rare occasions with small objects, no water seems to be displaced because 'surface tension' keeps the water in the container.

RESOURCES

1 A translucent container.
2 Water.
3 A variety of solid objects which will go into the container.
4 A 'wet area' to work in.
5 Protective clothing.

Lower object in gently

ACTIVITY W3

Pour some water into the container (about three-quarters full). Note the level of the water and watch what happens to the level as one of the objects is lowered gently into the water. Why does the water level rise? Is there more water in the container? (This is a difficult question for young children to answer correctly but it is still worth asking.)

Repeat the activity with different objects and amounts of water.

OUTCOMES

The water level rises since it is displaced by the immersed object. The increase in water level being equal to the volume of the immersed part of the object. Many young children will be convinced that, since the water level is higher, there must be more water in the container.

ACTIVITY W4

Activity W3 can be repeated but the level of the water can be marked before and after the object is placed in it either by marking the outside of the container with a suitable marker or by placing a paper strip against the container and marking the paper.

The different results can be recorded by drawing pictures of the container before and after adding the object.

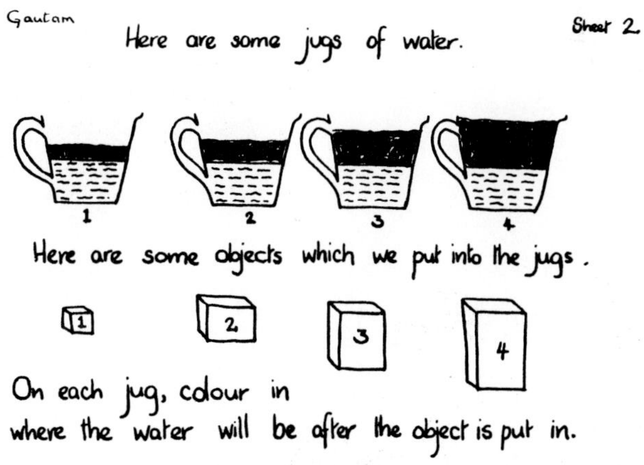

ACTIVITY W5

All of the above three activities can be taken a stage further by noticing what happens if the object is subsequently removed from the container and the drop in level noted.

Note The objects used should be at least sufficiently heavy to half-submerge in the water. This will exclude such materials as polystyrene and hollow objects like rubber ducks. If these have to be used then it would be necessary to push them under the water and this could give variable, and unreliable, results.

LINKING ACTIVITY: Story-telling

Aesop's Fables, 'The Crow and the Pitcher'. The story can be handled in a variety of ways from mime to a tape–slide presentation.

Our version of the story is included in Appendix 4. The story is usually told up to the point marked with an asterisk. The children can then suggest how Charlie solved the problem, using the knowledge gained from their previous experimental work.

Pupils carrying out mime

Objective: The pupils will be aware that big objects generally displace more water than small objects.

RESOURCES

1 A bucket, or similar container.
2 A basin, to stand the bucket in.
3 Several identical, translucent containers.
4 Several objects of different sizes but made from similar materials.
5 Water.
6 A 'wet area'.
7 Protective clothing.

ACTIVITY W6

Place the bucket in the basin and then fill it to the brim with water. Select one of the objects and lower it carefully into the water. Once the displacement of the water is completed lift the bucket carefully out of the basin and pour the water in the basin into one of the translucent containers. Remove the object from the bucket and lay it beside the container holding the water which it displaced.

Repeat the activity with the other objects until there is a sequence of containers and objects.

How much water does a large object push out of the way? How much water does a small object push out of the way?

Record the results by drawing the set of containers and objects.

OUTCOMES

The larger objects will displace a greater amount of water, provided they are completely immersed. If the objects that are being used tend to float then the results may be inconclusive. One way round this is to push each object completely under the surface using a pencil.

RESOURCES

1 Several identical, translucent containers.
2 Several objects of different sizes but made from similar materials.
3 Water.
4 A 'wet area'.
5 Protective clothing.

ACTIVITY W7

Half-fill each of the containers with water and mark the level of the water in each. Place one object in each container and mark the new level. Lift each object out of the water and place it in front of its container.

How much water does a large object push out of the way? How much does a small object push out of the way?

Record the results by drawing the containers, marking both the levels and the objects.

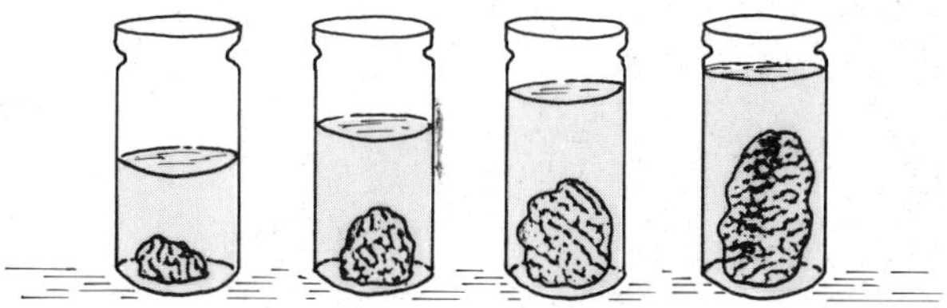

The larger the object, the greater the amount of water displaced

Objective: The pupils will be aware that some objects float and others sink.

RESOURCES

1 A bucket, or similar container.
2 Water.
3 A collection of objects, some which float and others which sink in water.

ACTIVITY W8

About half-fill the bucket with water then allow the children to place each object in the water in turn, noting which float and which sink.

The results can be displayed in two columns—'Floaters' and 'Sinkers'—either by writing the name or using a picture of each item.

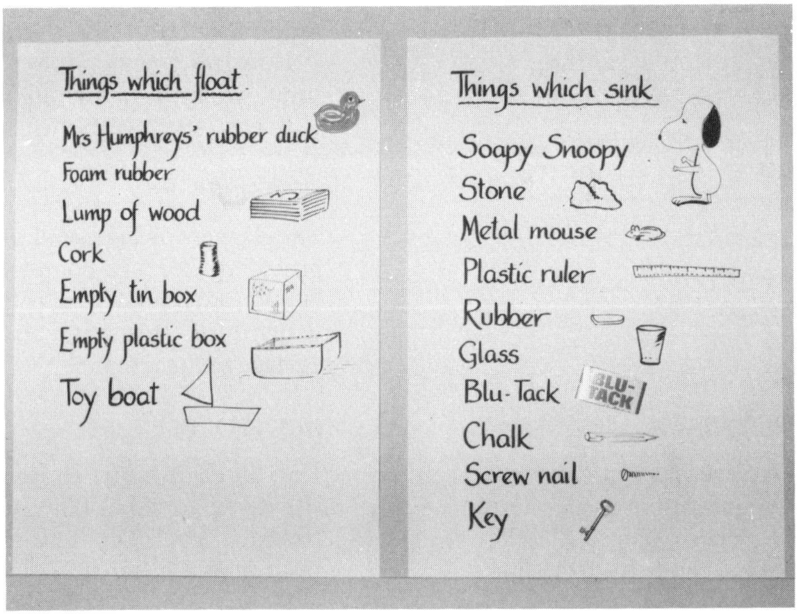

Wall display of 'floaters' and 'sinkers'

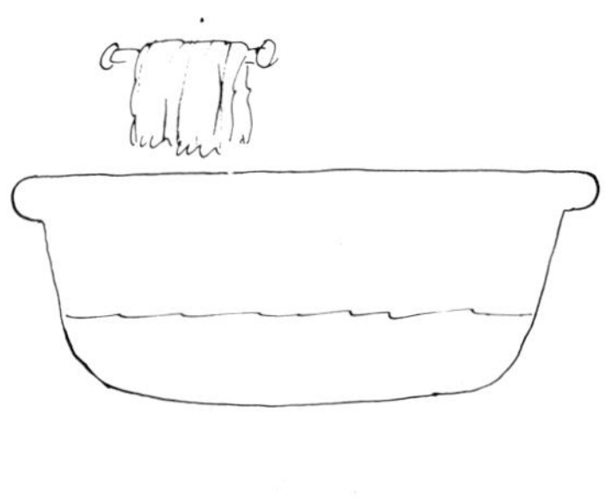

ACTIVITY W9

After carrying out the above activity suggest that the children bring in some objects of their own choosing so that they can work as 'detectives' and discover more things which float or sink.

Warning! Have a quick look at the objects which the pupils bring to make sure that they will not be damaged by water.

OUTCOMES

The results of Activities W8 and W9 will depend entirely on the objects selected. Remember that a hollow metal object will float while a solid one will sink and some woods, for example, ebony and Malayan teak, do not float so do not try to draw conclusions like: 'Metals sink and wood floats.'

heat

Heat and temperature

It is important to distinguish between 'heat' and 'temperature'. Heat is a form of energy and can be transferred from one object to another (usually with some loss in the process). The amount of heat an object contains depends on several things, the material the object is made of, the mass of the object and the temperature of the object. It follows that if two objects have the same mass and are made of the same material then the one with the higher temperature will contain the greater amount of heat. However, if the masses and materials are different then the temperatures of the objects will not be a guide to the relative amounts of heat they contain. For example, a red-hot pin will contain less heat (energy) than a kettle full of boiling water, although the pin would be at a higher temperature than the water. To illustrate this further think of what would happen if you wished to melt a hole in the ice on a frozen pond. The kettle of boiling water could well solve your problem but the red-hot pin definitely would not.

Temperature, then, is a measure of the degree of hotness of an object. Our sense of touch can give us some information about temperature over a limited temperature range, but it is not to be relied on too much. This is why we use thermometers when we want accurate information about temperature.

Heat energy can move from one object to another and will always move from the object with the higher temperature to that with the lower temperature. If the red-hot pin is dropped into the boiling water then heat will flow from the pin to the water. This amount of heat will be small and, while the temperature of the pin will drop considerably, the temperature of the water will not noticeably increase.

Melting and evaporation

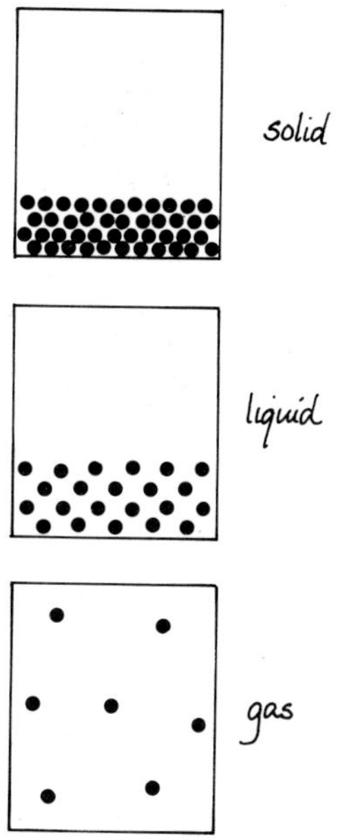

Molecular model for solids, liquids and gases

To understand the effects of melting and evaporation it is necessary to remind you of some basic ideas from your own early science lessons.

All substances are made up of molecules and the state of a substance depends on how these molecules are related to each other. In the case of a solid the molecules are close together and keep the same locations relative to each other, but they vibrate a bit around these locations. The energy of these vibrations can be looked upon as heat and the rate of vibration as temperature. In the liquid state the molecules have more energy and are no longer tied to a fixed location, while in the gaseous state they are much more free to move about.

It follows that the main difference between solid, liquid and gas is the amount of energy which the substance has locked up in its molecules. For a solid to turn into a liquid (to melt), energy must be supplied and for a liquid to turn into a gas (to evaporate), more energy must be supplied.

In the case of water evaporation, the resulting gas (water vapour) is invisible and the process is often thought of as the water 'drying up'.

The process of evaporation is, of course, extremely important biologically, when one considers the uptake of water by plants, for example. Water moves through plants, from the roots and up through the water-conducting vessels of the stem *en route* to the leaves where it is used not only in the metabolic processes of the plant but also in the process of transpiration—whereby it evaporates from the pores in the leaves into the atmosphere. In so doing it uses heat energy from the plant and this cools the plant.

As water is lost from the plant leaves by transpiration, more is drawn up in a continual stream from the roots. It follows, of course, that the hotter the atmosphere the more water the plant will lose in transpiration. If the rate of evaporation exceeds the rate at which water can be taken up through the roots then the leaf cells will lose too much water and will wilt. Jenny's droopy flowers in the garden were wilting because they were transpiring faster than they could replace the water from the dried up soil.

Note Do not attempt to explain transpiration other than perhaps to say that the water in the plants dries up in the heat and the plants need water to stand up and grow straight.

Evaporation of water from surfaces is also important as a means of losing heat for many animals. Human beings lose heat as a result of water evaporating from the sweat pores on the

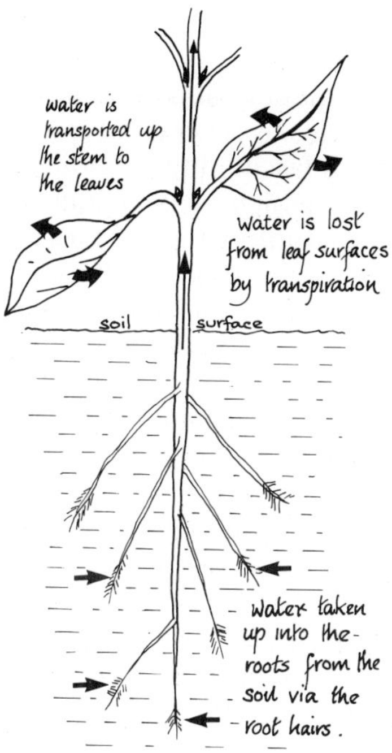

Water movement through the plant

surface of the skin and thus taking heat energy from the body. In order to assist this process when one is overheated, more blood is pumped to the surface vessels of the skin making it appear flushed. This also helps in that the hot skin in contact with the air will heat up the air and therefore cool down the body.

Many other animals lose heat by evaporation techniques as well. Dogs, for instance, don't have sweat glands so they can't lose heat in this way—instead they pant. Patch is panting in the story. What is happening is that the wet surface of his tongue is exposed to air and the dog exhales rapidly, blowing hot air over his tongue. The moisture on his tongue evaporates, taking heat energy from the animal in so doing, and this helps the animal to cool down.

Most animals, given the choice, will select to avoid overheating. Patch finds a cool place under a tree.

In investigating the effect of heat on plants or animals you must remember that time is an important factor and you will not get immediate results as you will with physical science activities. This can be a drawback with young children whose interest in any activity tends to wane after a short time. So that you can maintain interest we suggest that the children grow and investigate their own plants using fast-growing seeds and small 'Jiffy Seven' type peat pots. This has the added advantage of allowing the pupils to watch the growth of the seedlings prior to their being placed in an experimental situation and therefore the seed-planting activity should precede this by several days.

Note 'Jiffy Sevens' themselves are a fascinating phenomenon. They are compressed discs of peat which, when soaked in water, 'grow' into little pots full of peat into which the seed can be planted. They do not require a flowerpot and can be sat in a saucer of water and left. They are available from garden centres or seedsmen and are relatively inexpensive to purchase in packs of 30, or larger quantities if desired.

The following activities relate to these ideas and are intended to form a foundation on which a later understanding of them can be built.

In the story we see the effects of heat and evaporation on animals and plants as well as on the physical world.

Objective: The pupils will be aware that heat comes from the sun.

RESOURCES

1 A sunny summer's day.
2 Buildings or trees or some other large object which casts shadows.
3 Pupils.

ACTIVITY H1

Send the children outside to stand in a sunny part of the playground for a few minutes then move them into a part of the playground which is in shade. Do they notice any difference in how hot they feel? Where does the heat seem to come from?

This activity will work better if they face the sun or, at least, have the sunlight falling on their faces. Beware of allowing them to look directly at the sun as this could damage their eyes.

LINKING ACTIVITIES: Art/Weather recording

1 Draw 'sunny day' pictures.
2 Include sunshine, as part of the daily, or weekly, weather chart.

RESOURCES

1 A sunny summer's day.
2 Buildings or trees or some other large object which casts shadows.
3 Various metal objects, e.g. pot lids, coins, etc. two of each object will be required.
4 Pupils.

ACTIVITY H2

The metal objects are placed outside, one of each pair in a sunny part of the playground and the other in the shade. They are left for about half-an-hour. The children then return and touch each one of the pair. Which feels hotter? Where is the heat coming from?

When placing the objects in the sunny areas make sure that they will still be in the sunlight half-an-hour later.

With older classes discuss why there has to be two identical objects used in this test.

Note Activities H1 and H2 could be carried out inside the classroom on a sunny day if the sun shines through a window.

Objective: Pupils will be aware that a hot object in contact with a cold one will heat up the cold object and will, itself, cool down.

RESOURCES

1 Several blocks of metal. These could be either nuts (of the nuts and bolts type) or coins but the bigger the better.
2 A source of heat, e.g. the radiator in the classroom (provided the heating is on) or a cup of very hot water (*caution!*)

ACTIVITY H3

The objects are arranged in identical pairs then one of each pair is placed on (or in) the source of heat and left for around 10 minutes (until it is as hot as it will become). The cooler of the two objects is then touched by the pupil to estimate how hot it is. The same thing is done with the hot object. (Make sure it is not too hot.)

The two objects are then placed in contact and left for a minute or so. Each is now felt in turn. Has the hot one cooled down? Has the cool one heated up? Where has the heat from the hot one gone?

Note This activity ignores any heat lost to the air of the room but will still give a useful result.

DISCUSSION POINTS

If you are cold what do you do to warm yourself up? How is the classroom heated? Does the radiator cool down while it is heating the classroom?

(In most schools the heating is carried out by radiators which obtain heat energy from one of several sources, electricity, gas or hot water. The hot radiator supplies heat energy to the air in the room and in so doing loses heat itself. In other words it cools down but, of course, it is, in turn, re-heated by its source of energy. So, strictly speaking the radiator is always losing heat—cooling down—and at the same time having it replaced—heating up—at the same time. One way of illustrating this would be to turn off the source of the radiator's energy and note how the radiator cools down.)

RESOURCES

1 Half a cup of hot water, as hot as a pupil's finger can safely endure.
2 Half a cup of cold water.

ACTIVITY H4

Test the temperature of each amount of water by dipping a finger into each. Now pour the contents of one cup into the other. Test the temperature of the mixture with both fingers. What has happened?

Note This activity is harder for the pupils to understand since the two 'objects' lose their separate identities when they come in contact.

RESOURCES

1 A cold winter's day.
2 A pupil who has just been outside and whose hands are cold.
3 A pupil who has been inside and whose hands are warm.

ACTIVITY H5

The pupil with the cold hands should place one of his between the warm hands of the other pupil. After a few minutes compare the temperatures of the two hands of the pupil from outside. Why is one warmer than the other? Why do both hands heat up but one more slowly than the other? Where does the 'slower' hand get heat from? Do the warm hands become colder?

LINKING ACTIVITY: Poetry

'Cold day' poems.

Objective: The pupils will be aware that heat causes ice to melt.

RESOURCES

1 A small quantity of ice.
2 A saucer, or similar container.
3 A source of heat, e.g. classroom radiator.

ACTIVITY H6

Place the piece of ice in the saucer and the saucer on the source of heat. Watch what happens to the ice. The pupils should try to describe, either in writing or verbally, what they see happening. What is left in the saucer at the end of the activity?

Note If possible an identically sized piece of ice should be placed in a cold place (e.g. refrigerator) at the same time and its appearance compared at the end of the activity.

DISCUSSION

What happens to ice cream on a hot day?

Objective: The pupils will be aware that heat causes water to evaporate.

RESOURCES

1 Two saucers, or similar containers.
2 A small quantity of water.
3 A source of heat, e.g. the classroom radiator or the sun.
4 A wax crayon.

ACTIVITY H7

A small quantity of water is placed in each saucer and the size of the pool marked on the saucer by drawing round the edge using a wax crayon. One saucer is then placed on (or in) the source of heat while the other is left in a cool place out of draughts. The size of the water pool is marked at regular intervals on each saucer. The timing will depend on how hot the source of heat is, but should be such that a reasonably obvious difference in level occurs in the heated saucer. There should be little, or no, difference in the level in the unheated saucer.

Why has the water disappeared? Where has the water gone? These are difficult questions.

Note The concept of evaporation is too advanced at this stage—settle for 'the water has dried up' or similar phrases and ideas.

RESOURCES

1 A hot sunny day.
2 A puddle in the playground—this can be produced in several ways, e.g. wait for a shower of rain or use a bucket of water.
3 A piece of chalk.

ACTIVITY H8

Choose, or produce, a puddle in a sunny part of the playground. It is better if the puddle is very shallow and it must be in sunlight throughout the activity. Draw round the edge of the puddle with the chalk. Return at regular intervals and mark out the new puddle size.

Why does the puddle become smaller? Would the same thing happen on a dull, cold day? Try it on a dull, cold day.

The results can be recorded as 'Puddle Drying Charts' in the classroom, either in the form of a bar graph showing 'Size of puddle' (puddle diameter) or by drawing the actual puddle sizes on sugar paper.

Objective: Pupils will be aware that it is cooler in the shade.

Note The resources and activities for this objective are identical to those for 'Pupils will be aware that heat comes from the sun.' The only difference will be in the slant given to the discussion following the work. In effect this is a negative corollary to the first objective.

*LINKING ACTIVITY: **Language/Art***

Depending on the time of year, it may be possible to link in with holiday activities. For example, people sunbathing on beaches, people in the shade of umbrellas, cooling down in the sea, how hot the sand is on a sunny day, ice cream melting, etc.

Objective: The pupils will be aware that different animals use different techniques for temperature control.

DISCUSSION

Discuss the ways in which Patch and Jenny cool down.

This is not an experimental activity for both social and economical reasons. We don't really want the children running round the building to show that when they get hot they sweat and it is not all that possible to visit, for example, the Namib Desert to investigate the temperature-control mechanism in lizards!

Objective: Pupils will be aware that plants wilt when they become too hot.

RESOURCES

Each group of children will require the following resources.

1 Three similar seedlings in 'Jiffy Sevens' or small pots.
2 Water.
3 A 'hot-spot'—radiator or hot, sunny window sill.

Degree of wilting in different environmental conditions

ACTIVITY H9

Over a period of several days treat the three seedlings as follows:
Seedling 1—water regularly and leave in a cool, well-lit place in the classroom.
Seedling 2—do not water but leave beside seedling 1.
Seedling 3—do not water and leave at the 'hot spot'.

Observe the condition of the seedlings regularly, at least once a day and look for signs of distress. The children will not wish any of their plants to die so it is imperative that, once wilting occurs, a rescue operation is mounted (i.e. water the seedlings!).

The results can be recorded by the children producing a sequence of drawings to show how each plant looked each day.

A sound is produced when an object vibrates and the vibration has two characteristics which are important as far as the sound produced is concerned—frequency and amplitude.

Frequency

This is the rate of vibration and gives an indication of the pitch of the note produced. The higher the frequency the higher the pitch and, conversely, the lower the frequency the lower the pitch.

The human ear can detect frequencies from around 16 hertz (16Hz)—1 hertz is 1 vibration per second—to around 23 000 hertz (23 kHz). As the owner of the ear ages these limits come closer together, the higher frequencies especially becoming inaudible. Different animals have the ability to detect different frequency ranges, dogs, for example, having an upper frequency limit of around 30 kHz.

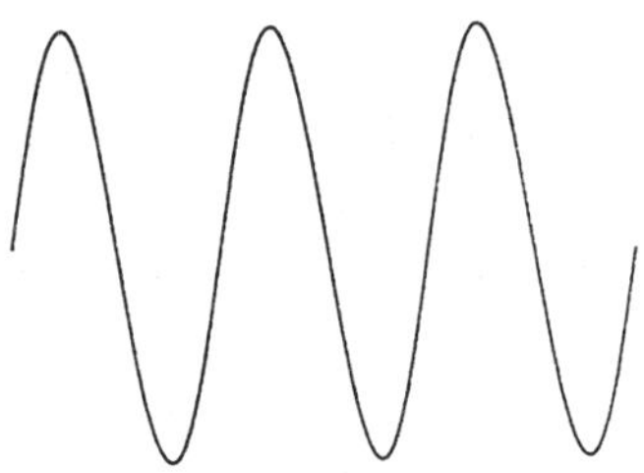

low note

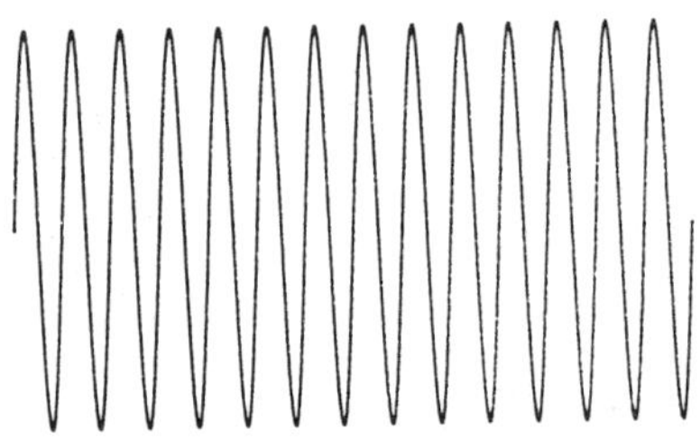

high note

The ability to distinguish the pitch of one note from that of another varies from person to person. Some people can rightly be claimed to be 'tone deaf' while others have what is known as 'perfect pitch' and can name correctly any note as soon as it is played. This ability is partly inherent and partly learned although, for most people, it takes considerable practice and experience to perfect. For this reason it is essential that pupils are encouraged to try to distinguish between different notes but you should not expect a great ability to be displayed by young children.

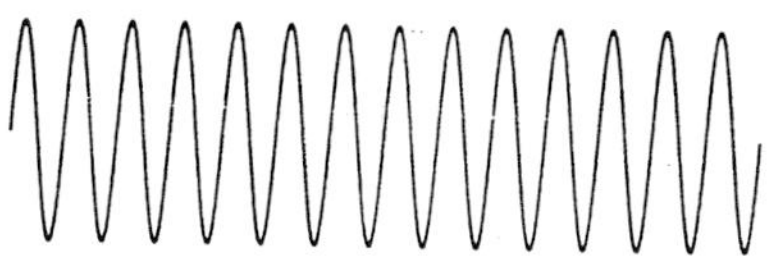

Amplitude

This is a measure of the size of the vibration and determines the loudness of a sound. The greater the amplitude the greater the loudness. Once again the ability to detect different loudnesses varies from person to person and even from ear to ear.

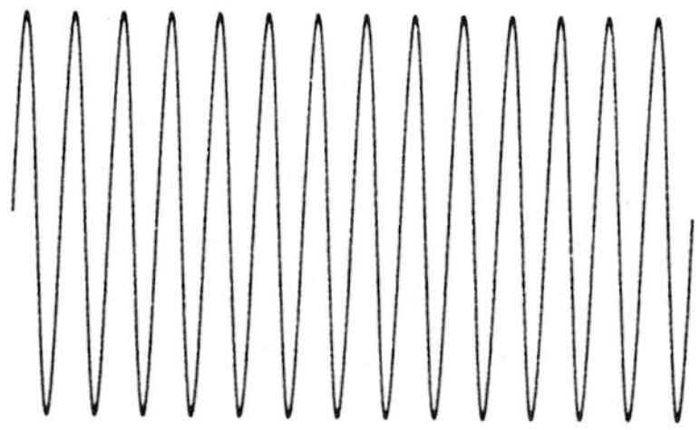

Waves

Sound vibrations behave like waves and travel in all directions and through all types of material—solid, liquid and gas.

When a sound which has been travelling through air meets a solid surface most of the energy is reflected and an echo is produced. If the solid surface is a considerable distance from the source of sound then the echo can be distinguished as a separate sound otherwise it may not be noticed or produce a reverberation effect. Sound travels at about 300 metres per second in air and so a separate echo is most likely to be noticed if the reflection surface is 100 metres or more from the source.

Note 1 Certain activities which deal with sound and its detection are covered in the chapter on senses.

Note 2 The linking activities for this chapter will most likely be related to the children's musical activities and could include making class lists of instruments which make the kind of sounds that the children are producing in their science activities.

Objective: The pupils will be aware that sound is produced by vibration.

RESOURCES

1 A selection of wooden, plastic or metal rulers—preferably 30 cm long.
2 Tables or desks.

ACTIVITY S1

Place the ruler overhanging the edge of the desk and hold it firmly down on the desk. Hit the projecting part of the ruler smartly. What happens to the ruler? What do you hear?

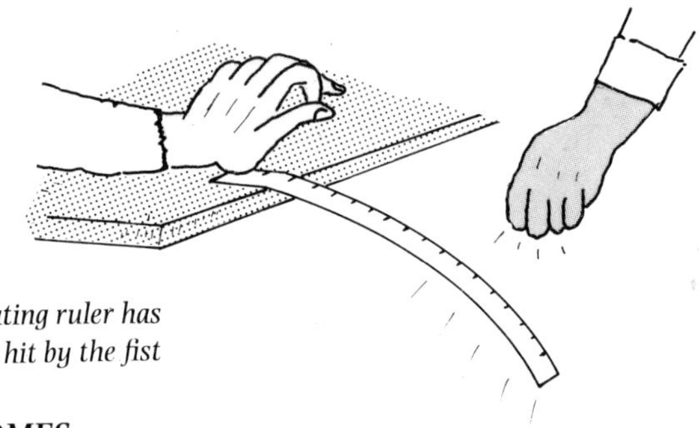

The vibrating ruler has just been hit by the fist

OUTCOMES

The ruler will vibrate and, provided it is held down very firmly on the desk, a sound will be heard. The note will die away as the vibrations gradually die down.

RESOURCES

Strips of paper about 20 cm long and 3 cm wide.

ACTIVITY S2

Fold the paper strip as indicated and tear a small hole in the folded end. Hold the paper between first and second fingers and place against the lips. Blow hard. What happens to the paper? What do you hear?

Making and using the folded paper whistle

OUTCOMES

The folded piece of paper will vibrate rapidly and a sound will be heard. The sound will tend to be loud and raucous so it might be worthwhile restricting this activity to one or two children at a time and removing the paper strips once the activity is over— unless you feel that you, or someone else on the staff, deserves a nervous breakdown!

RESOURCES

Bicycle bell, bell or chime bar.

ACTIVITY S3

Strike the bell and when it is sounding very gently touch the surface, just as Joanne does in the story. What do you feel?

OUTCOMES

The surface of the bell will vibrate and it should be possible to feel the vibrations. Unfortunately the process of touching the bell tends to stop the vibrations very quickly so it is essential to be very gentle and touch the surface only lightly.

RESOURCES

Tuning fork.

ACTIVITY S4

Strike the tuning fork and while it is sounding touch the end of the prong gently against the lips or the ear lobe. What do you feel?

OUTCOMES

Once again a tingling sensation will indicate that the tuning fork is vibrating. The feeling produced in the lips is quite odd and the children may be slightly apprehensive about this. If the 'touching' is heavy handed then the vibration will be stopped before it can be detected.

RESOURCES

1 Tuning fork.
2 Small bowl of water.

Prongs just touch water surface

ACTIVITY S5

Strike the tuning fork and while it is sounding dip the tips of the prongs into the water. What happens? Why?

OUTCOMES

This is quite a spectacular little trick when carried out correctly. The rapidly vibrating tips of the tuning fork will cause the water to vibrate and two things will be noticed. The most obvious will be a small fountain of water which will spray up between the prongs but, at the same time, the surface of the water will be covered in waves spreading out from the prongs.

Objective: The pupils will be aware that sound vibrations spread out in all directions.

RESOURCES

1 A large, empty playground.
2 A dry day.
3 A class of pupils.
4 A sound source, e.g. a bell or whistle.

ACTIVITY S6

Place one pupil with the sound source in the middle of the playground. The rest of the class stand round in a circle and a sound is produced. Everyone who can hear the sound raises a hand.

Repeat the activity several times with the circle of pupils being made larger each time. Does everyone hear the sound? What does this tell us about the way in which sound spreads out?

OUTCOMES

Everyone round the circle, and elsewhere, should hear the sound since sound spreads out in all directions just as the waves did in Joanne's bucket of water when she dropped the stone into it.

ACTIVITY S7

This is a modified form of 'Hide and Seek'. The class is allowed to hide anywhere within the playground, or other fixed boundary. The teacher then blows the whistle and the first pupil to reach the whistle is the winner and takes over the job of 'whistle blower'.

OUTCOMES

With this activity it should be possible to demonstrate that not only does sound spread out in all directions but it can also 'bend' round corners.

Note This last activity is obviously open to abuse. Someone is sure not to hear, or pretend not to hear, the whistle although the 'carrot' of being the next 'whistle blower' usually works.

Objective: The pupils will be aware that sound can be reflected.

RESOURCES

1 A playground or similar area with a wall at one end. Ideally the wall should be long, straight and high.
2 A source of sound of a high pitch—the young human voice will do.

ACTIVITY S8

Place the sound source about 150 m from the wall and facing it. The sound source should produce a short, sharp sound and the observers should listen carefully and record *everything* they hear. Do they hear one or two sounds?

If possible, the activity should be repeated with the source at a greater distance from the wall.

Sound source, wall and listeners positions to obtain an echo

Note This activity is almost identical to Joanne shouting at the mountain. Since the speed of sound is around 300 m per second there will be a 1 second gap between the original sound and the echo if the distance to the wall is 150 m. This gap is not sufficient to enable words to be made out but is sufficient if the original sound is short and high pitched. An echo should be detectable with shorter distances, even down to around 25 m, but the greater the distance the easier it is to make out the echo.

Objective: The pupils will be aware that sounds can be made with different pitch.

RESOURCES

1 A selection of wooden, plastic or metal rulers—preferably 30 cm long.
2 Tables or desks.

ACTIVITY S9

Place the ruler overhanging the edge of the desk and hold it firmly down on the desk. Hit the projecting part of the ruler smartly. What happens to the ruler? What do you hear?

Now alter the length of ruler which projects over the edge of the table and repeat the activity. What happens to the pitch of the note?

Repeat the activity several times, both lengthening and shortening the ruler. What happens to the pitch of the note each time?

OUTCOMES

This is an extension of Activity S1. The pitch of the note will become lower when the protruding part of the ruler is longer and a shorter vibrating section will produce a higher note. If the overhang is too great then the vibration will be too slow to hear and with too short an extension it may not be possible to hit the ruler hard enough to produce any vibration, so it pays to try this activity beforehand to make sure your classroom rulers will give the results you want.

RESOURCES

Strips of paper about 15 cm long and 3 cm wide.

ACTIVITY S10

Fold the paper strip as in Activity S2. Hold the paper between the first and second fingers and place against the lips. Blow hard. What happens to the paper? What do you hear?

Now alter the length of paper which protrudes between the fingers and blow again. What do you notice about the pitch of the note?

Repeat the activity with several different lengths of protruding paper. What happens to the pitch of the note?

OUTCOMES

In this activity the vibrating object is the protruding piece of paper and the longer this is the slower will be the vibration and therefore the lower the note produced. With extremely short sections of vibrating paper it may be necessary to blow very hard to produce a note.

Pupil blowing through paper strip

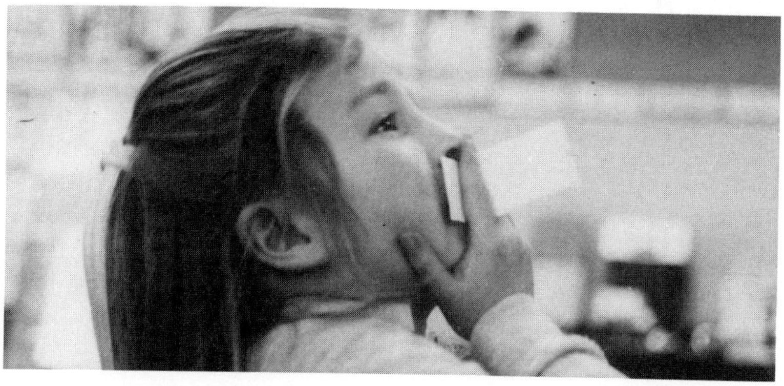

Objective: The pupils will be aware that sounds can be made which are loud or soft.

RESOURCES

1 A selection of wooden, plastic or metal rulers—preferably 30 cm long.
2 Tables or desks.

ACTIVITY S11

Place the ruler overhanging the edge of the desk and hold it firmly down on the desk. Hit the projecting part of the ruler smartly. What happens to the ruler? What do you hear?

Now repeat the activity but this time hit the ruler very hard. Is there any difference in the sound?

Repeat the activity a third time hitting the ruler very gently. What difference do you note this time?

OUTCOMES

Once again this is a modification of Activity S1. This time the vibrating length is kept constant and the amount of energy used to cause the vibration is increased and decreased. With a large amount of energy—a hard hit—the vibration will be vigorous and the sound loud while the opposite will be true when the ruler is hit gently.

RESOURCES

Strips of paper about 15 cm long and 3 cm wide.

ACTIVITY S12

Fold the paper strip as for Activity S2. Hold the paper between the first and second fingers and place against the lips. Blow hard. What happens to the paper? What do you hear?

Repeat the activity but this time blow very gently. Is the sound quieter or louder?

RESOURCES

1 Tuning fork.
2 A table or desk.

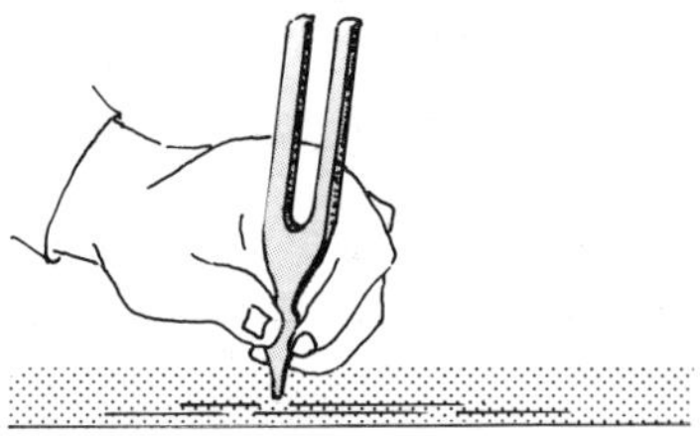

Hold the tuning fork by the handle. Don't touch the prongs

ACTIVITY S13

Strike the tuning fork gently and while it is sounding touch the handle end on to a table.

Repeat the activity but this time strike the tuning fork firmly. Is there any difference in the loudness of the sound?

Note The sound a tuning fork produces is not easy to hear when the tuning fork is held in the air since the prongs are not very efficient at making the air vibrate. If, however, the tuning fork is held with its handle pressed firmly against a large area of wood, or other solid substance, then the vibrations are transmitted to the wood which in turn causes a large amount of air to vibrate and the sound is easily heard.

moving

One of the basic purposes of science is to find out how things happen. When carrying out investigations to do this it is always very much easier if the number of possible variables is small. In this way any change can be directly attributed to a particular cause. When studying movement it is not easy to eliminate all the extraneous variables and, as a result, interpreting findings can be difficult. This may be why Archimedes was able to describe the reasons behind flotation around 700 BC but it was not until around AD 1700 that Newton was able to do the same thing for movement.

There are several inter-related concepts which are involved in the study of movement. We are going to look at: force, friction, momentum and inertia.

Force

A force is perhaps best defined simply as a push or a pull. This push or pull does not need to have visible or material connection with the object which it is pushing or pulling. For example, gravity and magnetism can both cause objects to move without any visible connection to the object.

Friction

This is a special example of a force. It is always present when there is movement, or the tendency to movement, between two surfaces which are in contact. Friction tends to prevent or reduce movement between surfaces.

Sometimes friction is essential. Imagine trying to walk if there was no friction between the sole of your foot and the ground, or trying to drive a car if there was no friction between the wheel and the ground. A very close approximation to this occurs when walking, or driving, on ice.

On the other hand, friction can be a disadvantage. For example, friction between the wheels and the axle in a car uses up energy and makes it more difficult to move the car. If the friction is not reduced by lubrication it may be impossible for the car to move.

Generally, when trying to gather information about movement the effects of friction mask the results being looked for and it is usual in this case to try to reduce friction as much as possible.

Momentum

This is a measure of the amount of energy a moving object has, as a result of moving. A stationary object has no momentum.

The greater the mass of a moving object the greater the momentum. Equally, the greater the speed of the object, the greater the momentum.

Let's apply our idea of reducing the variables to a minimum and carry out a 'thought' experiment. Which would do you the least damage if it hit you, a bus travelling at 10 miles per hour or a fly travelling at 10 miles per hour? Obviously, the bus—the more massive object has the greater momentum.

Alternatively, which would do you the least damage, a fly travelling at 10 miles per hour or one travelling at 100 miles per hour? This time the object with the higher speed has the greater momentum.

Inertia

This is the tendency objects have to stay as they are. An object which is not moving is difficult to start moving while one which is already moving is difficult to stop. In both cases a force is required to alter the state the object is in initially.

The activities

The activities listed in this section are, once again, intended to give the pupils a 'feel' for the ideas and concepts which they will learn and appreciate much later in life. When they have come to terms with these concepts, at a later stage of their development, the children will be better equipped to cope with the problems of technology and design which are so necessary in dealing with the demands of our present age.

Note Hector and his truck are obvious candidates for the experimental work in this section. A wooden truck with wheels can easily be built or obtained and a large felt Hector made using the pattern shown in Appendix 5. Obviously measurements can be made for the pull required to move the truck with Hector and without Hector.

Objective: The pupils will be aware that to make a stationary object move a force is required.

RESOURCES

1 A marble, or other small, hard round object.
2 A small, motorless toy car. It should have no inbuilt means of propulsion of any kind.
3 A level, very flat floor.

ACTIVITY M1

Place the marble on the floor so that it is not moving. How can you make it move? Try pushing it? What happens?

ACTIVITY M2

Repeat the experiment using the small car.

RESOURCES

1 A large wheeled toy or toy truck—one like Jane's would be ideal.
2 An area of level smooth playground.

ACTIVITY M3

Place the truck in the playground and challenge anyone to move it without touching it. What must they do to make it move?

OUTCOMES

There is no way in which you can make any of the objects move unless you use a force of some description. Even if some 'big blow' in the class succeeds in moving the truck using lung power a force has still been used. If the 'blower' blows against someone's hand the force will be felt.

Objective: The pupils will be aware that the amount of movement depends on the size of the initial push.

RESOURCES

1 A marble, or other small, hard round object.
2 A small, motorless toy car. It should have no inbuilt means of propulsion of any kind.
3 A level, very flat floor.

ACTIVITY M4

Place the marble on the floor so that it is not moving. How can you make it move? Try pushing it? What happens? How can you make it move faster?

ACTIVITY M5

Repeat the experiment using the small car.

RESOURCES

1 A large toy truck or some form of large-wheeled toy.
2 A small toy car.
3 A level, very flat floor.
4 A 'pusher'. This is to ensure that both vehicles are given the same amount of push at the same time. Any strip of wood will do.

ACTIVITY M6

Place the truck and the car side by side and place the 'pusher' behind them and touch both. Now push hard on the 'pusher'. Which one travels the greater distance?

The 'pusher' is used to propel the car and truck

ACTIVITY M7

Push the small car and see how far it travels. Now try to push the truck so that it travels the same distance. Which one requires the bigger push?

Note The large truck will have to be pushed several times before the correct size of push is found.

A pupil pushing the truck

OUTCOMES

In each case it is obvious that the greater the push given to the same object the faster and/or further it will travel. When the objects are different then the results will be different. Generally speaking, the heavier object will be slower and move a shorter distance than the lighter object when given the same push, and will require a larger push to make it move the same distance or at the same speed as the lighter one. It may be that you will find the occasional exception to this if the friction at the wheel axles of the small car is too great, so check the activity before you let the children try it.

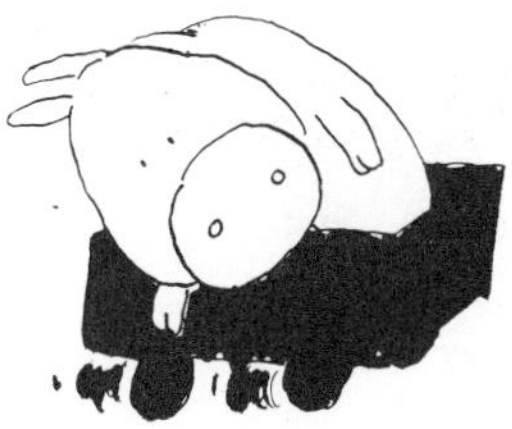

EXTENSION ACTIVITY

Encourage the children to play a game of marbles. This incorporates the ideas and the findings of Activities M1 to M7 and allows them to increase their experience and have fun at the same time.

Objective: The pupils will be aware that to make a moving object stop a force is required.

RESOURCES

1 A marble, or other small, hard round object.
2 A small, motorless toy car. It should have no inbuilt means of propulsion of any kind.
3 A large, heavy ball—a football will do.
4 A level, very flat floor.

ACTIVITY M8

Roll the marble rapidly across the floor. Ask a pupil to stop it. What must he do to stop it? What does he feel on his hand?

ACTIVITY M9

Repeat Activity M8 using the small car.

ACTIVITY M10

Repeat Activity M8 using the football.

OUTCOMES

There should be no difficulty in discovering that a force is required to stop any moving object. The activities will work better if the objects are launched fairly enthusiastically. If the child trying to stop the object misses then it will continue until it reaches a wall and this will supply the necessary stopping force.

Objective: The pupils will be aware that some surfaces can supply the force necessary to slow down or stop a moving object.

RESOURCES

1 A smooth, well-polished block of wood, or a toy with a smooth surface.
2 A table with a smooth, well-polished surface.
3 A piece of sugar paper.
4 A piece of sand-paper.
5 A piece of carpeting or rough cloth.
6 The force-measuring device described in Appendix 6.

ACTIVITY M11

Fix the end of the force measurer to the wooden block then pull the block at a steady speed across the polished table. Make a note of how strong the pull is.

Now pull the block, at a steady speed, across each of the other surfaces in turn, noting the force required in each case.

Do all the surfaces try to stop the block moving with the same force? Which surface allows the block to move most easily? Which surface makes it most difficult to move the block? Make a list showing the order from 'Easiest' to 'Most difficult'.

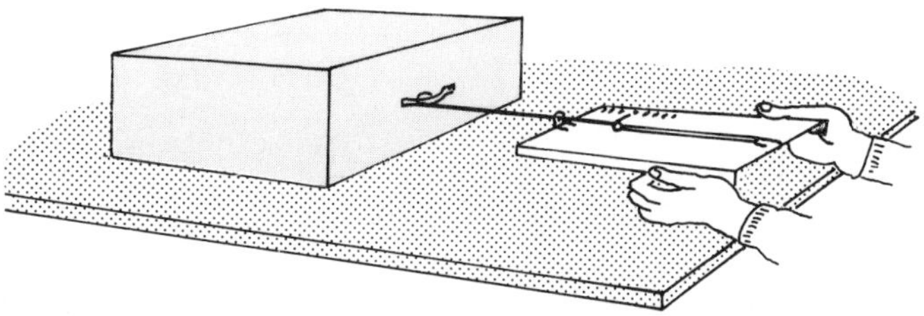

Force measurer in use

Block being pulled along with force measurer

RESOURCES

1 A smooth, well-polished block of wood, or some toy with a smooth surface.
2 A table with a smooth, well-polished surface.
3 A piece of sugar paper.
4 A piece of sand-paper.
5 A piece of carpeting or rough cloth.

ACTIVITY M12

Give the block a good push to start it sliding across the table. Measure, or mark, how far it travels on the smooth surface.

Try the activity again using the sugar paper then using the sand-paper followed by the carpeting. Which surface slows down the block the most? Which one slows it down least? Once again make up a list showing 'Worst at stopping' to 'Best at stopping'. Is this list similar to, or the same as the one discovered in Activity M11? It should be!

RESOURCES

1 A wheeled trolley (one like Jane's will do).
2 A piece of playground which has a dry, smooth surface running into a puddle of mud. (If you don't have a muddy puddle the class will be delighted to make one for you. All you have to supply is some water and a quantity of soil.)

ACTIVITY M13

Give the trolley a push across the smooth part of the playground and see how far, and easily, it moves. Now give it the same sort of push, but this time aim it at the mud puddle. Does it move easily through the mud?

OUTCOMES

In Activity M11 the force measurer should indicate a greater force being required to move the block over the rougher surface. Depending on your choice of carpet and the weight of the block you might find that the carpet offers a greater resistance than the sand-paper or vice versa.

Activity M12 is an alternative way of producing similar results to Activity M11. It is well worth approaching the same concept from different routes in order to reinforce the ideas and emphasize the results. Remember not everyone 'sees' the world in the same way and while one child may well appreciate Activity M11 another might only spot what we are driving at through Activity M12.

Activity M13 is a repeat of what happens to Hector. The mud should slow down the truck quite quickly.

Note If you persevere with Activity M13 and you and your class successfully complete it then you should award yourself the Order of the Bath—you'll most likely need it!

*LINKING ACTIVITY: **Poem/Games/Language***

1 *Song of the Train* by H. Worsley-Benison.
2 Written and recorded accounts of a class Grand Prix with toy cars.

wheels

One of the biggest problems primitive man had to overcome was moving heavy objects over rough, or for that matter smooth, surfaces. Perhaps the earliest way of solving this problem was to place round branches or tree trunks under the heavy object and roll it over them. The greater the diameter of the branch the easier it is to move the object over rough ground.

The next step is an obvious one. Cut a slice off the end of the tree trunk, pin it through its centre onto the heavy object and you have invented the wheel!

There are various factors which determine how helpful a wheel is going to be in the 'moving business'—for example, the size of the wheel and friction.

Wheel size

A small wheel will stick in indentations and ruts which a large wheel would ride over. However, the bigger the wheel the heavier and more expensive it is so you try to match the size of the wheel to the job it has to do. For example, the wheels on a super-market trolley are not very big since they are really meant to be used on extremely smooth floors. When the same trolley is taken out into the car park the wheels are totally inadequate and the resulting difficulties often produce frayed tempers.

Friction

Friction can be a benefit and a drawback as far as wheels are concerned. If there is no friction between the wheel and the

Small wheels will stick in surface indentations

ground then it will not be possible to predict the direction of motion. The wheel will slip and skid at random just like a car on an icy road. If there is friction between the wheel and the axle it will be difficult to turn the wheel and all the benefits will disappear.

Objective: The pupils will be aware that wheels make it easier to move an object.

RESOURCES

1 A heavy, flat object, e.g. a book.
2 A reasonably smooth table top.
3 Several round pencils or pieces of dowelling.
4 The force-measuring device described in Appendix 6.

ACTIVITY WH1

Attach the force-measuring device to the book and find how much force is needed to drag the book across the table. Now place the pencils under the book and pull the book along. Measure the force this time. Is it more or less? Do rollers (wheels) help things to move?

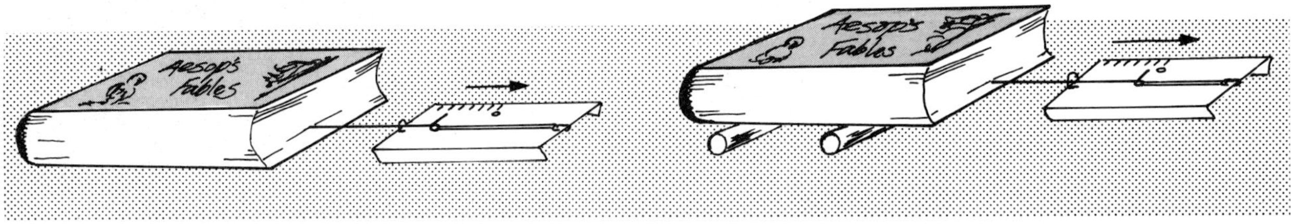

Force required to move book is less when rollers are employed

RESOURCES

1 A toy car with wheels that can easily be removed. (You will find that many of the children have cars like this at home—they did not start out life with detachable wheels but wear and tear produces the effect we are looking for.)
2 A floor or table top.

ACTIVITY WH2

Give the car a push across the table top and see how far it travels. Now remove the wheels and give it the same strength of push again. Does it travel as far?

ACTIVITY WH3

Give the car a small push across the table top. Mark how far it travels. Now take the wheels off and try to give the car a push so that it will travel the same distance as before. Is the push bigger or smaller than before?

Objective: The pupils will be aware that wheels do not work well if they sink into the surface over which they are moving.

RESOURCES

1 A toy trolley with wheels about 10 cm in diameter.
2 Some stones or other heavy object to act as a load.
3 A piece of hard playground surface.
4 A piece of very soft grass (or soil) surface.

ACTIVITY WH4

Push the trolley, complete with load, across the hard surface. Now try pushing it over the soft surface. Is it harder to do or easier to do?

Try the activity again but this time look carefully at the wheels. Do the wheels leave a track on the grass? Do they leave a track on the hard surface?

Tracks left by truck in soft grass

OUTCOMES

The tracks left in the soft surface show how the wheels have sunk in and a greater push is needed to make the truck move.

When the truck is standing still on the soft surface the wheels sink in because of the weight of the truck and its load. If you now try to move the truck you have to push the wheels out of the hollow they have made. As the truck moves along it is continually making a new hollow which it has to be pushed out of. It is just as if you were pushing the truck up a slope all the time.

On a hard surface the wheels do not sink in so there is no upward 'slope'.

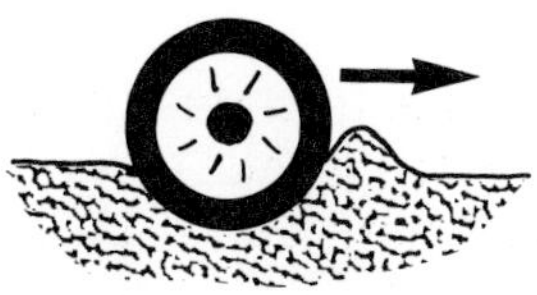

Wheel in hollow—'hill' in front must be overcome

Objective: The pupils will be aware that wheels do not work well on highly-polished surfaces.

RESOURCES

1 A toy car with wind-up or friction-drive motor.
2 A track made of sugar paper.
3 A very smooth surface like Formica or ice.

ACTIVITY WH5

Wind up the car a small amount and release it on the sugar paper track. Measure how far it moves.

Now wind up the car to exactly the same amount then release it on the highly-polished surface. Measure how far it moves this time. Compare the two distances. Why are they different?

ACTIVITY WH6

Repeat Activity WH5 but this time look carefully at the wheels on the car each time. Do they spin round more when on the smooth surface?

OUTCOMES

In order to make the car move forward a force must be exerted on the ground. This must obviously happen at the point where the wheels touch the ground. The wheels will only 'grip' the ground if there is friction between them and the surface. With a smooth, shiny surface the friction is so small that the wheels get little or no grip and movement is limited.

LINKING ACTIVITY

Again the children will be anxious to bring in their own toys to try out these activities and this can offer valuable extension material as well as being lots of fun. Cars with different sizes of wheels and motors will appear and can be compared, discussed and raced.

appendix 1 LIGHT-TIGHT BOX

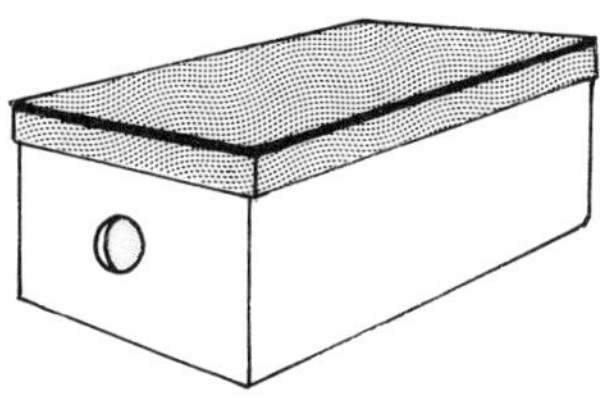

Light-tight box with peep hole

You will require:

1 A box with a removable, tight-fitting lid. A shoe box or one similar in design is ideal.
2 Masking tape.
3 A pair of scissors, a sharp knife or a scalpel.

Remove the lid from the box and cut a hole about 2 cm in diameter in the middle of one end.

Replace the lid and look through the hole with your eye as close as possible to the box. If there are any chinks of light leaking through holes, except between box and lid, cover the holes over using masking tape. Several layers of tape may be needed and it will help if the tape is coloured black.

appendix 2 COLOUR MASK

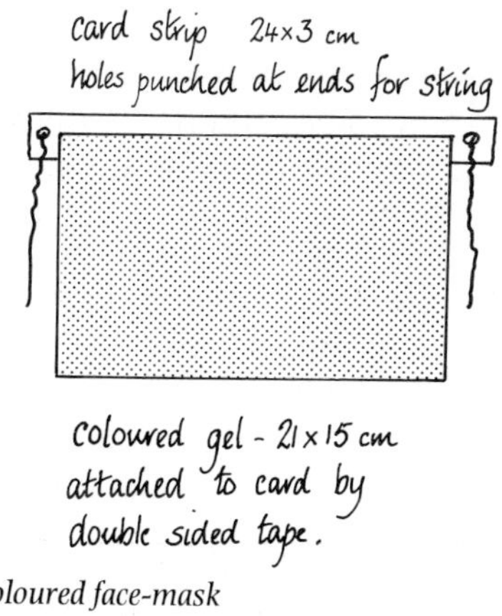

Coloured face-mask

You will require:

1 A strip of card about 24 cm long by 3 cm wide.
2 A piece of coloured acetate about 21 cm by 15 cm. The best material for this is the coloured gels used for stage lighting. You may be able to obtain this from a local drama group or theatre, or from a theatrical supplies company. Alternatively, a photographic retailer may be able to help. The best colours to use are 'primary' red, 'primary' blue or 'primary' green.
3 Masking tape.
4 String or elastic.

Attach the coloured acetate to the card strip using the masking tape. Punch holes in either end of the card strip and attach the string or elastic.

appendix

3 CAT AND MOUSE MASKS

You will require (for each mask):

1 A piece of card about 20 cm by 20 cm.
2 String.
3 Scissors.

Enlarge the designs shown here on to card. There are several ways of doing this.

(a) Use an episcope and project the outline on to a wall. Stick the card on the wall and draw round the outline. The image size can be altered by moving the projector back or forward.

(b) Trace the outline on to a piece of OHP acetate. Place the acetate on the OHP and project the image on to a wall. The position of the image can be altered using the adjustable mirror in the head of the OHP and the size of the image can be changed by moving the OHP back or forward.

(c) If a lot of masks are being made then the easiest procedure is to enlarge the outline, using (a) or (b) above, on to a spirit duplicator master then run-off copies using the spirit duplicator. Most spirit duplicators will copy on to thin card if you don't set the pressure too high and feed each sheet by hand.

Colour-in the mask—the children will thoroughly enjoy doing this. Punch holes and attach string.

appendix

4 THE CROW AND THE JUG

It was a very hot summer. There had been no rain for weeks and weeks. All the ponds and rivers had dried up and the ground was hard. The animals in the countryside were all *very* thirsty.

Some of the birds had even died.

Charlie Crow was a fine handsome bird but even he was miserable because he was so thirsty. He flew here and there just hoping for one beakful of water, but he could not find a drop.

'Oh dear, oh dear!' said Charlie, 'If I don't get some water soon I shall die.'

And that was true. Many of his friends had already died. He was very sad.

As he sat on a tree, trying to shelter from the bright sunlight, he spotted something in the distance. It was a cottage with an open window and, what do you think was on the window sill? A jug!

'Great!' said Charlie, 'People often have water in jugs. I'll fly over and have a look.'

He landed on the window sill with a 'plop', looked around—there was no one in the kitchen so he jumped up onto the rim of the jug and looked in. Right down in the bottom of the jug was sparkling fresh, clear, water. But, oh dear, he couldn't reach it. Poor Charlie! What could he do? He stretched his neck down as far as he could but it was no use. The water was too far away. He was so disappointed he could have cried.

By this time, some of his friends had joined him on the window sill. They were thirsty too. They discussed the problem.

Robert Robin and Sammy Sparrow felt that they should be able to peck a hole in the side of the jug. 'Get the strongest bird here,' said Sammy. 'You try yourself, Charlie.'

But poor Charlie was too weak.

Even when they all joined in, and pecked at the jug it would not break.

Morton the Magpie joined them on the ledge.

'Having a bit of bother?' he asked. Morton always had an answer for everything.

'We're trying to help Charlie here to get the water in that jug,' said Robert the Robin.

'Simple—just push it over. Out of my way and I'll show you!' Morton pushed and pushed, but the jug would not move.

'Perhaps if we threw stones at the jug it would break,' said Tommy the Thrush. 'That's how I open my lunch when I'm eating snails.'

All the birds started to pick up pebbles from the garden path and throw them at the jug. They made a great deal of noise but still the jug wouldn't break.

While all this was going on, poor Charlie just sat and watched. Suddenly he had an idea. 'Stop!' he ordered. 'We are all tiring ourselves out when we should be using our heads to think this out.'*

'Look at the litter of stones lying about on the window sill! Now listen everyone, and do as I say. Pick them up, one at a time and drop them gently into the water.'

The other birds thought he was a bit mad but they did as they were told. One by one, the robin, the sparrow, the thrush, the magpie and Charlie, dropped stones into the water and what do you think happened?

The water in the jug rose nearly to the rim. All those pebbles had pushed it up to the top and there was lots of water for all the birds to drink.

'What a clever fellow Charlie Crow is!' they called. 'He has saved our lives. Three cheers for Charlie Crow!'

appendix

5 MAKE YOUR OWN HECTOR

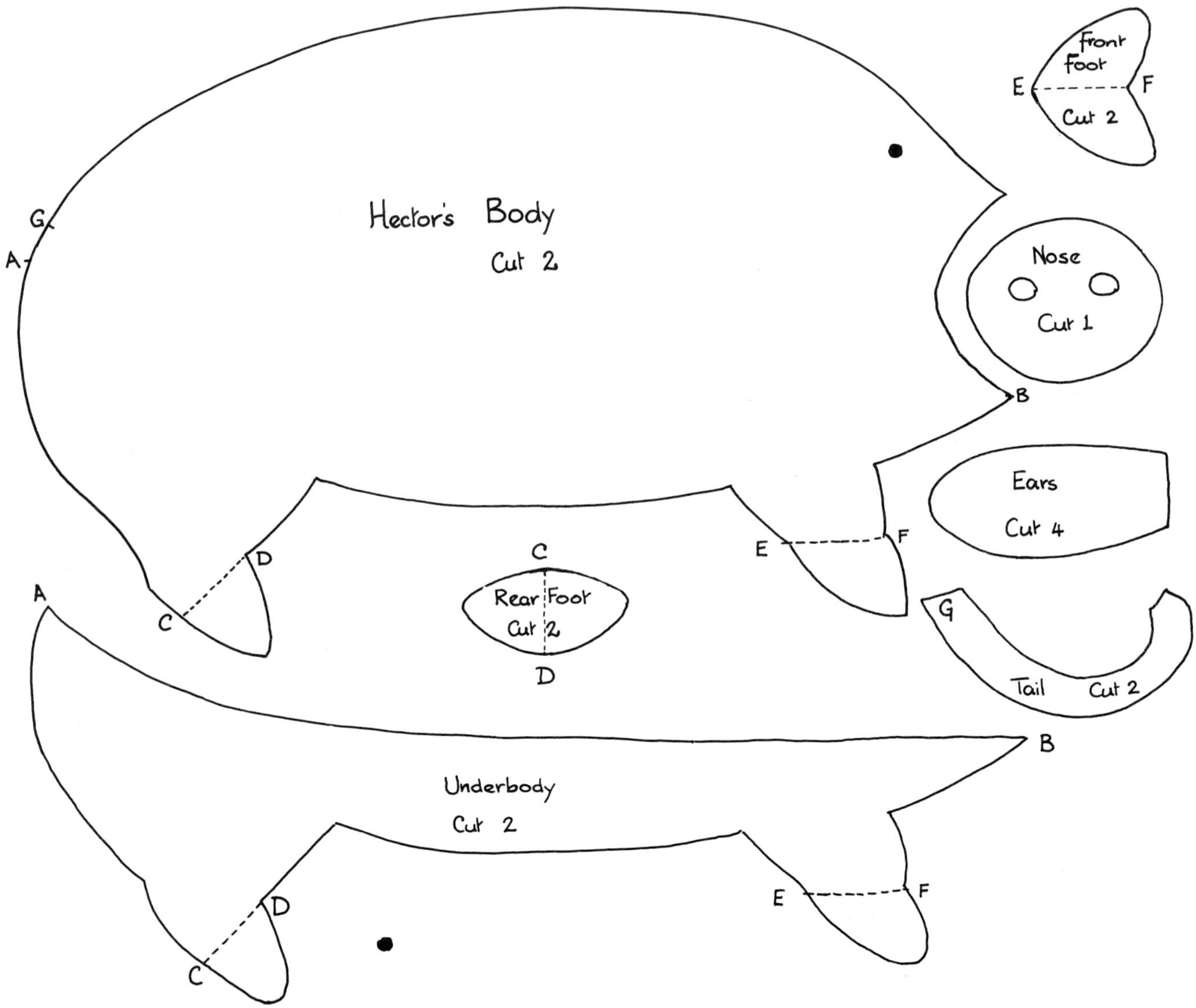

appendix

6 FORCE-MEASURING DEVICE

You will need:

1 A piece of stiff card about 20 cm by 12 cm.
2 A piece of wire about 20 cm long. This is best obtained from a wire coat hanger—the kind used by dry cleaners.
3 2 paper clips.
4 An elastic band.

Score the card about 1.5 cm in from each of the long edges and fold it back to about 45 degrees.

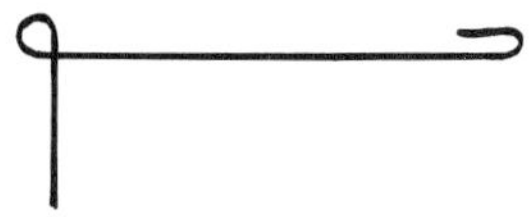

Bend the piece of wire as shown.

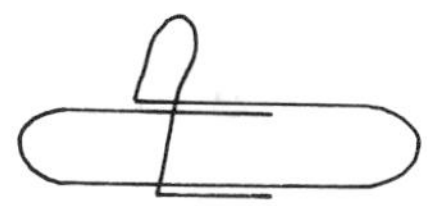

Bend up the end of one paper clip.

Push the bent paper clip on to the bottom of the card and the other on to the top.

Thread the elastic band through the loop on the wire and over the top paper clip.

Slip the hook end of the wire through the loop at the bottom clip.

Hold the force measurer upright and mark the position of the pointer. This indicates zero force. Using a ruler mark equal divisions of, say, 1 cm from there down. These will not correspond to any particular force but will give an idea of how the force being measured is increasing.

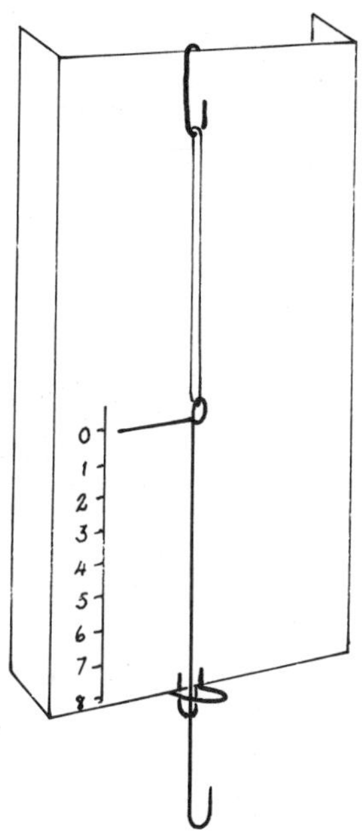

Force measurer

index

Page references in ordinary type are to activities.

Page references in **bold type** are to background information.